CHINA'S OFFENSIVE IN EUROPE

Philippe Le Corre

and

Alain Sepulchre

TRANSLATED BY SUSAN EMANUEL

BROOKINGS INSTITUTION PRESS
Washington, D.C.

Library of Congress Cataloging-in-Publication data

Names: Le Corre, Philippe, 1964– author. | Sepulchre, Alain,
    author.
Title: China's offensive in Europe / Philippe Le Corre and Alain
    Sepulchre ; translated by Susan Emanuel.
Other titles: Offensive chinoise en Europe. English
Description: Washington, D.C. : Brookings Institution Press,
    [2016] | Includes bibliographical references. | Description
    based on print version record and CIP data provided by
    publisher; resource not viewed.
Identifiers: LCCN 2015045074 (print) |
    LCCN 2015040687 (ebook) | ISBN 9780815727996 (epub) |
    ISBN 9780815728009 (pdf) | ISBN 9780815727989 (pbk.)
Subjects: LCSH: International business enterprises—China. |
    Investments, Chinese—European Union countries. | China—
    Foreign economic Relations—European Union countries. |
    European Union countries—Foreign economic
    relations—China.
Classification: LCC HF1604.Z4 (print) | LCC HF1604.Z4
    E1842313 2016 (ebook) | DDC 338.8/895104—dc23
LC record available at http://lccn.loc.gov/2015045074

Typeset in Sabon
Composition by Westchester Publishing Services

CONTENTS

Contents

This book seeks to introduce the reader to the phenomenon of growing Chinese direct investment in Europe, from 2009 to 2015. To understand the context for that investment, it is useful to review developments in China's domestic situation, in China's relations with its neighbors, and in China's relations with the United States.

The emergence of China on the world stage is a subject that preoccupies numerous academics, economists, and strategists—whether in government, think tanks, or the media—on both sides of the Atlantic. Especially in the United States, Chinese economics, finance, politics, security, and societal issues are dissected and interpreted on virtually a daily basis. There is a parallel phenomenon within China, as experts at major universities and think tanks analyze the various facets of America's politics, economy, and society—and increasingly of Europe's as well.

Since Xi Jinping assumed power as general secretary of the Chinese Communist Party (CCP) in 2012 and subsequently as state president, China has experienced its share of geostrategic tensions and political and economic challenges. They include ongoing frictions with Japan over portrayals of World War II history and disputed land features in the South and East China Sea, contentious relations with Southeast Asia and India, a growing rivalry with the United States, street protests calling for bolder electoral reforms in the Chinese Special Administrative Region of Hong Kong, protests in Taiwan against closer ties with Xi's China, and growing economic uncertainty. From the early 1990s to 2012, the Chinese economy enjoyed frenetic growth of almost 10 percent per year on average, making China the world's second largest economy after the United States, but that growth is now slowing. Total debt, including the financial sector, has nearly quadrupled since 2007,[1] to the equivalent of 282 percent of GDP. The year 2007 was when the Chinese government introduced a stimulus package to compensate for the financial crisis in the rest of the world. China's demographic trends are worrying, with its elderly population swelling and its working-age population shrinking. Moreover, the People's Republic of China is profoundly inegalitarian: the economic miracle has not benefited everybody. While the 2015 Forbes China Rich List contained the names of more than 300 U.S. dollar billionaires, the GDP per person that year remained almost five times lower than that of the United States and Europe.[2]

The Chinese political system, which the Communist Party intends to dominate indefinitely, is now evolving, but not in the direction of some kind of democratization. Instead, Xi Jinping and his colleagues have chosen a diehard nationalism that includes a whiff of Confucian tradition and culture, an anticorruption campaign aimed at tens of thousands of officials at all levels of the power structure (party, state, army, and state-owned enterprises), and an official "Chinese Dream" of a national renaissance, the Chinese counterpart of the American Dream. There have been attempts to build this slogan into a propaganda tool to accompany China's international drive.

Corruption is a widespread phenomenon in China, linked to economic opportunity, with some party officials enriching themselves from the financial manna of exports and the economic "miracle" of the past thirty-eight years. Xi appears to have concluded that it was

out of control. Corruption had evidently reached a stage that Xi Jinping and the team that has surrounded him since 2012 deemed a
serious threat to the legitimacy of the CCP. With more than 600
million Chinese online as of 2015, the CCP cannot be insensitive to
criticism, especially in the era of social media—Weibo, WeChat, and
Baidu, specifically—that, despite censorship and firewalls, fostered
a new form of online popular condemnation. This anticorruption
campaign touches not only Chinese citizens but also some foreign
corporations, which are accused of having made illegal profits.

The anticorruption campaign initiated by Xi Jinping, which will
continue until the 19th Party Congress in the fall of 2017, has trig-
gered animosity within the Chinese elite. On the one hand, outside
analysts frequently present Xi as the first strongman of China since
Deng Xiaoping, the so-called chief architect of the policy of reform
and opening to the outside world, who died in 1997; on the other,
Xi's reformist vision sometimes seems hesitant. The government's
management of the stock market crisis in 2015 and early 2016 gave
rise to criticism from many small investors, as was to be expected,
but also from opponents of the party's main line both inside and
outside the CCP. As in many other countries, the economy in China
presumably is a key factor influencing social stability.

Abroad, China is active on many new fronts. It has launched a
vast program of economic development outside its borders, starting
with the "One Belt, One Road" initiative (an elaborated version of
the new Silk Road concept) proposed during trips by President Xi
to Kazakhstan and Indonesia in the fall of 2013 and often reaf-
firmed during official speeches and regional tours in 2014 and 2015.
One component of this mega-idea will take the form of a network
of overland roads and railways, oil and natural gas pipelines and
facilities (the "Silk Road Economic Belt"), that will stretch from
Xian in central China through the Chinese Special Autonomous
Region of Xinjiang to Central Asia, ultimately reaching as far as
Europe. The other component, the 21st Century Maritime Silk Road,
is envisaged as a network of new port and coastal infrastructure

capabilities extending from China through South and Southeast Asia all the way to Africa and the Mediterranean Sea. Promoted at the highest levels of the Chinese government, and overseen by the State Council's National Development and Reform Commission, the Ministry of Foreign Affairs, and the Ministry of Commerce, the initiative will extend well beyond infrastructure construction as it will also include efforts to promote greater financial integration and international use of China's currency, the renminbi; to create, through fiber-optics, an "Information Silk Road" linking regional information and communications technology networks; and to lower barriers to cross-border trade and investment in the region, among other ideas.

In April 2015, Xi Jinping visited Islamabad and concluded the trip with the announcement that China would invest $46 billion in infrastructure, much of it for an "economic corridor" encompassing roads, railways, and pipelines along 3,000 kilometers to the Pakistani port of Gwadar, which is intended to give China land access to the Indian Ocean. If all the elements of this plan are realized, Chinese investment in Pakistan will greatly exceed total U.S. investment in the country.

These announcements have been accompanied by the creation in Beijing of a $40 billion Silk Road Infrastructure Fund and by the $100 billion Asian Infrastructure Investment Bank (AIIB), which in the spring of 2015 registered no fewer than fifty-seven countries among its founding members, including European countries (the United Kingdom, Germany, France, Italy, and Poland) and traditional allies of America in the Asia Pacific region (South Korea and Australia). Many questions remain about this new bank, which will both cooperate and compete with the World Bank, the International Monetary Fund (IMF), and the Asian Development Bank—organizations until now controlled by the West and Japan. The rationale for the AIIB is simple: failing to obtain a major voice in the governing bodies of institutions such as the World Bank, China decided to create a new multilateral development bank. China achieved a diplomatic coup by attracting American allies, though not the United

States itself, as founding members of the bank. Lately, it also achieved its goal of increasing its stake in the traditional international financial institutions when the U.S. Congress cleared the way for a 2010 IMF quota reform package. It also became a member of the London-based European Bank for Reconstruction and Development in December 2015. Now China's credibility in Asia, the most crucial region for the new bank, depends partly on the AIIB's success.

China's capacity to invest can be seen on other continents as well. Since the end of the 1990s, China's leaders have pursued the idea that to sustain economic growth, Chinese business must expand internationally. State-owned enterprises that benefit from the gigantic financial power of the Chinese government ($3.56 trillion in reserves as of September 2015) have received orders to invest abroad.[3] Chinese private enterprises (sometimes facilitated by the Chinese diaspora) have joined in. Asia, Africa, Latin America, Australia, and even the United States are all experiencing the phenomenon of Chinese business internationalization. Between 2002 and 2014, the annual flow of Chinese investment abroad went from $2.1 billion to $130 billion (according to the Heritage Foundation/American Enterprise Institute's China Global Investment Tracker).[4] Chinese Premier Li Keqiang estimated this amount at $103 billion in 2014.[5]

Western firms seeking access to the Chinese market, however, continue to face obstacles. They include the absence of transparency and the weak protections for intellectual property in China. Many foreign corporations that had made China one of their principal terrains in the 1980s and 1990s are now reexamining their presence there. The annual reports of the European Chamber of Commerce (Eurochamber, with 1,800 members) and the American Chamber of Commerce in China (AmCham China, with 3,500 members) both reached the same conclusion: the Chinese market is no longer what it once was. AmCham China's 2015 white paper lists reforms to strengthen the rule of law, open markets, standardize norms, and improve protection of intellectual property as priorities for the chamber's advocacy efforts. All are flaws of the current system.

The Eurochamber's 2014 position paper offers a somber commentary: "In China, the golden age is ending for European corporations, for the country is on its way to closing its window of opportunity in order to equilibrate its economy. . . . Unless Chinese management makes and maintains reforms, there is a true risk that the economic miracle will dwindle."

In other words, the twenty years that enabled multinational corporations to get rich in the "fat" Chinese market are being gradually replaced by a period of "lean cows" for investors, especially European ones. Although the market for most goods and services is growing, foreign firms are facing a less hospitable environment in accessing it. It is hard for them to ask for better access because they are no longer truly welcome. With the slump in Chinese growth, and sometimes also for political reasons, the chances are good that priority will be given to local entities. The doors have closed in the case of many public markets, in particular with respect to certain sectors—construction, infrastructure, and telecommunications— henceforth reserved for local enterprises or subject to antimonopoly laws. The rules of the game are changing in China, and another economic strategy is emerging. The Chinese government sees innovation as a possible lifeline, but China's financial efforts to boost research (funding for which represented 1.7 percent of GDP in 2014, compared to 2.9 percent in the United States) have not been sufficient to make China a "creative and inventive economy."[6] A McKinsey Global Institute report in October 2015 suggested that "to realize consensus growth forecasts—5.5 to 6.5 percent a year—during the coming decade, China must generate two to three percentage points of annual GDP growth through innovation, broadly defined. If it does, innovation could contribute much of the $3 trillion to $5 trillion a year to GDP by 2025. China will have evolved from an 'innovation sponge' absorbing and adapting existing technology and knowledge from around the world, into a global 'innovation leader.'"[7]

Meanwhile, the government's agenda is to invest abroad in order to fuel the Chinese economic engine, and notably to utilize the liquidity accumulated over the course of the past several decades to acquire the technologies that are still lacking in China. This desire also spurred the 2007 creation of the China Investment Corporation, the largest Chinese sovereign wealth fund, which today manages $575 billion and has bought shares in many international technology companies.

The mutual distrust between China and the United States has gradually mutated into an open rivalry between the world's two largest economies. Although there is a permanent dialogue on many economic issues, it can be acrimonious at times when it comes to cybersecurity, intellectual property, currency matters, or market access. There is also a sense of competition in international and security affairs. Under Xi Jinping, China is clearly stating that it wants to play a larger role within the United Nations[8] and other international organizations. China also seeks to dominate Asia, which has been the object of a U.S. "rebalance" since 2011. In military terms, it is clear that the United States continues to lead at the strategic level: in 2014 the U.S. defense budget reached $581 billion (3.3 percent of GDP), as opposed to China's $129.4 billion for defense (1.2 percent of GDP). The two military capacities are not comparable, as Pentagon experts recognize, but the Chinese navy in particular has benefited from massive budget increases.[9]

Beyond the military domain, China is also trying to use its soft power in many parts of the world. Has it been fruitful? As Professor Joseph Nye of Harvard University writes, "Much of American soft power is produced by civil society, running from universities and foundations to Hollywood studios and pop culture." While China tries to establish its military might (particularly in the South China Sea), Chinese efforts at wielding soft power are far from successful: "China makes the mistake of thinking that the government is the main instrument of power. But in today's world, information is not scarce but attention is, and attention depends on credibility. For all the efforts to turn Xinhua and Central China TV into competitors of the BBC and CNN, there is little international audience for brittle propaganda."[10]

The Chinese fascination with the United States has not yet translated into large-scale investments in the industrial sector, although investments that do not have national security implications, and so are exempt from review by the Committee on Foreign Investment in the United States, are relatively easy to complete. According to a May 2015 report by the Rhodium Group, Chinese investments enjoyed a veritable leap between 2010 and 2014, reaching $46 billion for 1,583 subsidiaries throughout the United States.[11] Examples include Yunhua Chemical's $1.85 billion investment in a factory close to the Mississippi River in Louisiana, Lenovo's $2.9 billion purchase of a Motorola factory in North Carolina, and Shandong Tranlin Paper Group's $2 billion establishment of a production facility in Richmond, Virginia, in addition to other investments in IT and the automotive and rail industries. On top of these industrial projects, there is a strong presence of Chinese buyers of real estate, particularly in New York and California. This situation, which will necessarily have an impact on Sino-American relations, is reminiscent of the expansion of Japanese investments in the United States in the 1980s (though without the strategic rivalry).

Especially during crises over hacking and cyber-sabotage, distrust of China remains strong in Washington, and the electoral period may not be the best time to analyze Sino-American relations calmly. Some see China as a strategic competitor of the United States in the Asia Pacific region, some see it as a destroyer of jobs. Increasingly, it is the scapegoat of choice for an anxious American political class, an anxiety sometimes fed by well-documented cases with alleged strategic implications, such as the aborted purchase of the oil group Unocal by the China National Offshore Oil Corporation in 2005 or of 3Leaf, a cloud computing company, by Huawei in 2011. Even Shuanghui International's 2013 acquisition of the agro-food giant Smithfield was almost blocked by pressure from interest groups.[12] In short, American and Chinese strategic interests collide in a great number of domains, pushing China to turn its attention more widely to another part of the Western world, one with perhaps a less confrontational view of China: Europe. Because of the multiple challenges they have faced over the past few years, including the debt crisis, falling currencies, rising unemployment, and de-industrialization, European political elites have been somewhat more pragmatic than their American counterparts toward China, rapidly opening the door to more significant and strategic investments from 2008 on. Hence the subject of this book: China's economic offensive in Europe.

ACKNOWLEDGMENTS

This book, part of the Brookings Order from Chaos project, could not have been written without the generous assistance and wise advice of many people. The authors would like to thank for its support the Foreign Policy program at Brookings Institution, including the Center on the United States and Europe (CUSE) and the John L. Thornton China Center. Inside or outside Brookings, colleagues who took time to brainstorm and offered critiques included Richard Bush, Robert Daly, David Dollar, Feng Zhongping, François Godement, Matthew Goodman, Charles Grant, Fiona Hill, Martin Indyk, Bruce Jones, Robert Kagan, Kemal Kirişci, Cheng Li, Kenneth Lieberthal, Liu Ming, Michael O'Hanlon, Alar Olljum, Steven Pifer, Jonathan Pollack, David Shambaugh, Constanze Stelzenmüller, May-Britt Stumbaum, Strobe Talbott, Harold Trinkunas, Gudrun Wacker, Thomas Wright, Xu Mingqi, Yu Qiao, and Zhang Jian. At Pew Research Center, we would like to acknowledge Richard Wike, Bruce Stokes, and their excellent research team, whose work has been incredibly useful to us.

Invaluable support at Brookings was given by Gail Chalef and Rachel Slattery (Communications); Laura Mooney and Sara Chilton (Brookings Library); Andrew Moffatt (CUSE associate director); and Vassilis Coutifaris and Caitlyn Davies (CUSE coordinators). As editors of the Foreign Policy blog *Order from Chaos,* Jeremy Shapiro and Anna Newby always provided guidance. Tsing-Yi Wang (in Paris) and Joldoshbek Osmonov, Hao Xue, and Yimei Zhang (in Washington) were all fantastic research assistants.

We are particularly indebted to Kenneth Lieberthal, Susan Lawrence, Matteo Garavoglia, Michael O'Hanlon, and Jonathan Pollack, who kindly took time to review parts of the book and provided essential recommendations.

At Brookings Institution Press, the authors thank for their guidance and assistance Valentina Kalk, Bill Finan, and Janet Walker.

At Westchester Publishing Services, we benefited from the great editing skills of Angela Piliouras and Marjorie Pannell.

Finally, we would like to thank our wives, Jiajia and Myra, for their constant support, and our children, Emerence, Charles-Alexandre, and Gustave, for being such great multicultural human beings with a real taste for "fusion" food.

INTRODUCTION

EUROPE AS A STRATEGIC PRIORITY

Despite the disillusionment that accompanied China's first wave of investments on the European continent, prior to 2008–09,[1] Europe in 2016 has become a preferred playing field for China in the West. For several years now Europe has attracted both state-run and private Chinese enterprises looking for investment opportunities, despite the historical, geographic, legal, linguistic, societal, and cultural complexities of investing in Europe.

The European Union today has also become China's chief commercial partner, with €467 billion in bilateral trade in goods in 2014 (and a trade deficit of €137 billion in favor of China). China is thus the EU's most important trading partner after the United States, a situation that is of signal interest to officials at the European Commission in Brussels. But a major new subject garnering media attention in the years to come may well be Chinese foreign direct investment (FDI) in Europe. Unlike trade and tourism, investment is about long-term commitment, and Chinese companies are looking for a stable, legally secure environment. Whereas during the first decade of the twenty-first century there was little significant Chinese

1

investment in Europe, the figures since 2010 show a real investment surge. According to a report published jointly by the law firm Baker and McKenzie and the New York–based Rhodium Group, Chinese investments in Europe went from $6 billion in 2010 to $55 billion in 2014.[2] And in 2014, annual investment doubled to $18 billion. "Europe is now into its sixth year of consistently high levels of Chinese FDI with investment averaging $10 billion annually over each of the past four years," the report stated.[3] Bruegel, a Brussels-based economic think tank, estimates the distribution of Chinese outbound foreign direct investment (OFDI) flows as follow: 19 percent of total Chinese OFDI took place in Europe (stock: $13.9 billion) and 13 percent in North America (stock: $11.4 billion),[4] which has also become an important recipient. It should be noted that the United States remains by far the main holder of inward FDI in the EU: at the end of 2012, the United States held close to two-fifths (39 percent, or $1,683 billion) of total EU FDI stocks from the rest of the world, followed by Switzerland, Japan, Canada, Brazil, Russia, Singapore, Hong Kong, and China. Chinese FDI increased by 44 percent in 2012, but China held a relatively small share of the total, around 3 percent.[5] In France, for example, where there has been some resistance on the part of some local officials and communities, the share of Chinese FDI is still only around 2 percent of the total, with only 13,000 jobs created as a result of Chinese investments, according to French government figures.[6] Time matters: the first significant Chinese industrial investment contract in France was signed less than ten years ago, although the number of new projects has been on the rise ever since.[7]

The current wave of substantial and increasing Chinese investments in Europe has accelerated as a result of the 2008–09 global economic crisis, which ravaged several countries (for instance, Greece, Portugal, Ireland, Spain, Cyprus) and buffeted major European economies, including those of the United Kingdom, Germany, and France, the three largest EU economies as well as other recipients of Chinese FDI. Ranking fifth, after Portugal, Italy is also a particularly eloquent case: in 2014 alone, China invested more than $3.5 billion in various Italian projects, especially in the energy sector. The Italian companies with Chinese investors as owners number 322, give work to 17,800 people, and produce $9.2 billion (€8.4 billion) of Italy's GDP.[8] In 2015 the ChemChina Group bought up the Italian tire manufacturer Pirelli, one of the largest in the world and a well-known brand among Formula One racing enthusiasts.

Unsurprisingly, Chinese state banks—the China Development Bank, the Export-Import Bank of China, but also the Bank of China, the China Bank of Construction, and the Industrial and Commercial Bank of China (ICBC)—gave the starting signal for acquisitions five years ago by opening branches throughout Europe. Today, ICBC, China's largest commercial bank, maintains twelve European branches and anticipates more. Its global banking services are aimed primarily at a Chinese clientele interested in European products. As a result of credit facilities, a large number of properties have been acquired, including commercial ones, for example in France, where the managing director of ICBC, Victor Xiao, proudly proclaimed in 2014 that "no fewer than twenty châteaux in the Bordeaux region have been bought by our intermediary."[9]

Chinese banks serve as intermediaries between state-owned enterprises (SOEs) and investors throughout Europe for projects ranging from participation in key infrastructure projects (water, gas, port, and airport installations) to buying up corporations as varied as the British restaurant chain Pizza Express or the German manufacturer of machine tools Putzmeister, to the purchase of important structures, such as Madrid's landmark Edificio España, acquired from Grupo Santander in 2014 for $284 million (€260 million).

Until 2012, the sums in play were modest. One can speculate as to the difficulties that prevented the wave of Chinese investments from taking root faster in Europe. Companies such as ZTE, Haier, Huawei, or COSCO were among the pioneers but were content with opening sales offices and enjoying some commercial success, thanks to competitive products. ZTE and Huawei, for example, both managed to win important contracts with major European telecommunications operators such as Vodafone, BT, or SFR in 2006–10. But despite the triumphant statements from European agencies charged with attracting foreign capital, few long-term industrial installations or job-creating units were established by China until recently.

They were perhaps influenced by negative stories, shot through with cultural misunderstanding, such as the episode of the forty-one-kilometer stretch of the Warsaw A2 highway linking Warsaw and Berlin. In 2009, the state-owned China Overseas Engineering Group (COVEC) was awarded a contract to build the stretch through an EU tender. As a result of mutual incomprehension, the Chinese project was delayed and, two years later, having failed to deliver, COVEC had to retreat. The Polish government canceled the contract on the pretext of having to follow environmental laws about protecting animal species threatened with extinction. COVEC never got over this failure, which caused a stir in Beijing at the time and remains one of the worst experiences of a Chinese enterprise in Europe. On the other hand, sometimes the Chinese demonstrate an originality that seems blind to the host country's history and business practices: in Denmark, they offered to finance a tunnel linking the country with Germany, without taking into account the obvious strategic aspects of such infrastructure. A common cultural obstacle was that Chinese negotiators had learned their trade in China (or in Africa, where Chinese companies became active in the late 1990s), which led to embarrassing and illegal situations, such as the local head of a telecom group foolishly wanting to offer money to help convince a potential client.

THE COMING WAVE OF CHINESE INVESTMENT

What has changed to explain China's new craze for Europe? First, the Chinese central government began encouraging this investment drive toward Western countries only a few years ago: under the previous Chinese leadership of President Hu Jintao, Beijing gave priority to the development of the domestic Chinese economy, which led to the massive deployment of capital in Africa and Latin America, two important suppliers of natural resources. The "European wave" is clearly a continuation of China's "Zou Chu Qu" (走出去) or "Going Out" policy designed by Beijing in the late 1990s to encourage the international expansion of Chinese companies. Until 2008–09, Chinese entrepreneurs believed that European markets were too complex and overly regulated. On numerous subjects, a Sino-European dialogue of the deaf had long dominated, as all who were involved in transactions during the first decade of the twenty-first century could attest. For a long time, Chinese business executives could not adjust their practices to meet European standards and habits. In the Chinese business world, trust is like a treasure chest that cannot be opened with Western logic. Trust is the fruit of a long learning process, the product of social relations—if not familial and geographic ties, or those linked to shared student life. In Chinese enterprises, at headquarters or at subsidiaries abroad, the climate is often one of distrust between colleagues. Competition is also at play, with the promise of a yearly bonus for each successful yet obedient employee. Between Chinese and European businesses, intercultural differences likely played also a much larger role in damping down relations than people recognized. Now, the situation is starting to improve as investors realize the mix of cultures is sometimes a good thing. It will take time before the battalions of Chinese graduates of European universities and business schools find their place in this grand game of dominoes, but a handful of Westernized Chinese executives have been recruited. Some are even running European companies just acquired by Chinese investors, or (more rarely) the European subsidiaries of major Chinese corporations.

Diplomatically, relations with Europe have been rather good for the past decade—as long as controversial subjects are not raised. Chinese leaders have recently attached a special importance to European institutions. As pointed out in a recent report celebrating forty years of EU-China diplomatic relations, there is a permanent Sino-European dialogue in many fields.[10] Both China and the EU increasingly use the term "partnership" to define their relationship: in 2015, they celebrated four decades of diplomatic relations by announcing an "EU-China Comprehensive Strategic Partnership."[11] In addition to economic issues, the EU-China summit in June 2015 in Brussels took up new areas of concern, such as cooperation on security and in the fight against terrorism. The European Commission and the Chinese government signed a joint summit declaration on this occasion, and for once, Premier Li Keqiang, who was attending, publicly expressed a wish that Greece remain in the euro zone.[12] Interestingly, President Xi Jinping, who had a successful state visit to the United Kingdom in October 2015, also made a bold comment, pointing out that the UK as an important member of the EU "could play a more positive and constructive role in promoting in-depth development of China-EU relations."[13] Such statements are highly unusual for leaders of a regime that officially states it "does not interfere in other countries' politics."[14] Xi Jinping wanted to make the point that China cares a great deal about the EU's future.

Now that many European governments are clearly looking for more cash and foreign investors, the Chinese leadership has decided to engage Europe on multiple fields, especially economics and finance. Every Chinese state or high-level visit now includes an important delegation of Chinese CEOs and business leaders. A growing number of Chinese—mainly private—companies have started to adapt to the European way by hiring more Europeans and adopting EU standards. This has become more obvious since China launched its "One Belt, One Road" (OBOR) initiative focusing on infrastructure investments, and showed a strong interest in building or rebuilding some of the current European infrastructure—energy plants, utilities, airports, ports, highways, and the like. China even offered to take part in the European Commission's investment plan, raising expectations of a potential incorporation of OBOR's European destinations within a broader Chinese strategy.[15]

European FDIs are part of China's new policy, which also includes trade, culture, the media, education, and "people-to-people" exchanges. The Chinese leadership, which is nurturing contacts with individual European leaders through bilateral visits or multilateral forums, such as the "16 + 1" summit,[16] is keen to increase political and diplomatic exchanges with Europeans. During 2015, no fewer than twenty bilateral summits took place between Chinese and European leaders. Beijing believes that rivalry and competition with the United States will continue, as demonstrated during the past year: the strong participation of European countries in the China-backed Asian Infrastructure Investment Bank, as well as the multiple Sino-European joint declarations and memoranda of understanding on the future OBOR were ways for China to spread its wings in the western direction as twelve countries were negotiating the U.S.-designed Trans-Pacific Partnership (TPP), which was finally agreed to on October 5, 2015. One could also underline that China worries about another, not-yet-signed major potential trade agreement, the Transatlantic Trade and Investment Partnership (TTIP), still under discussion between the United States and the EU. Both trade deals could potentially isolate China, which has therefore initiated several major economic projects involving Europe in the fields of infrastructure or finance, including the internationalization of the renminbi, which in late 2015 was included in the IMF's basket of reserve currencies.

Many publications by eminent academics, among them Thomas Christensen's *The China Challenge: Shaping the Choices of a Rising Power* (W. W. Norton, 2015) and Lyle Goldstein's *Meeting China Halfway: How to Defuse the Emerging U.S.-China Rivalry* (Georgetown University Press, 2015), have reported in detail on the often tumultuous relations between China and the United States. Several books, including Howard French's *China's Second Continent* (Virago, 2014), have studied the growing Chinese presence in Africa. The role of China in Latin America also interests many scholars, among them R. Evan Ellis, author of a book titled *China in Latin*

America: The Whats and Wherefores (Lynne Rienner, 2009) or Kevin P. Gallagher, who wrote *The Dragon in the Room: China and the Future of Latin American Industrialization* (Stanford University, 2010). Relations between China and Europe, on the other hand, especially those connected to China's outbound investments, have thus far received little academic treatment. This book therefore seeks to address the lacuna by examining relations between these new partners, the Chinese and the Europeans, focusing mainly on investment flows, but also raising strategic issues.

China's Offensive in Europe aims to describe China's effort to spread its wings in Europe economically since 2009. Chapter 1 explores, through numerous examples and portraits, China's relationship with both the EU as a whole and a number of key European countries (Germany, France, the United Kingdom, Italy, Greece, Spain, Portugal), and how these countries are reacting to the deployment of Chinese investments. Chapter 2 reviews some of the sectors targeted by Chinese investors (including SOEs and private companies), from real estate to energy, including railways and automobiles. Chapter 3 then analyzes the most influential and global Chinese business groups, such as Huawei and Haier, and distinguishes various categories of corporations. Chapter 4 deals with relations between investors and Chinese finance, which is essentially state-run, and how that relationship affects their European businesses. Chapter 5 tackles the immense intercultural challenges that, twenty years after Japan's wave of foreign investments in the United States and Europe, surround the international deployment of Chinese investments. Certain issues appear to be common to most Chinese investors when they look abroad, including differences in the legal environment and in specific laws governing imports and exports, labor, and corporate behavior; marked differences in employer-employee relationships and in corporate decisionmaking; the quality and quantity of corporate communications, including communications with the press, shareholders, staff, and leading political figures; and relations with headquarters or with the Chinese government. On this last subject, chapter 6 describes the specific phenomenon of the interconnectedness of Chinese politics and business and what impact it may have on building a long-term corporate presence in Europe. Chapter 7 details the difficulties experienced on the ground by China as it attempts to improve its international image, one of the principal obstacles to the expansion of its companies in Europe and in the Western world in general. Closing the itinerary, chapter 8 looks at China as a new member of the international community, and offers thoughts for reflecting on in the future.

ONE

CHINA'S ENTRY INTO THE EUROPEAN MARKET, 1985–2015

FIRST STEPS

In 2015, the European Union and the People's Republic of China celebrated forty years of diplomatic relations. The pre-Tiananmen China of Deng Xiaoping (China's paramount leader from 1978 to 1992) signed its first agreement on cooperation with the former European Economic Community in 1985, principally on customs and tariff questions having to do with markets access. The relationship was formalized ten years later with the publication of a "Communication" on China by the European Commission.[1]

Both the EU and the PRC have changed a great deal in the past four decades. The EU now has twenty-eight members, and China is the world's second largest economy, as reflected in the bilateral trade and in the no fewer than sixty yearly bilateral dialogues between Beijing and Brussels on subjects ranging from education and training to science, culture, urban planning, food, youth, technology,

11

intellectual property, and sustainable development. Over the years, joint projects have included the creation of a business school, the China-Europe International Business School (CEIBS, now completely separate from the EU), and forums for professionals such as the China-EU Managers Exchange Training Program, which trained 400 Chinese and European executives. Overall, however, the relationship is mainly about trade. Between 1995 and 2013, EU imports from China increased elevenfold, while over the same period exports multiplied 10.5 times. Today, China is the EU's second largest trading partner, after the United States.[2] In 2001, China's accession to the World Trade Organization (WTO) provided a boost to the country's openness.

China has published various reports defining its relationship with the EU, including one in April 2014 titled "Deepen the China–EU Comprehensive Strategic Partnership for Mutual Benefit and Win-Win Cooperation" that was intended to set the tone for the next ten years, after an examination of recent history and the international and national context, especially as it bore on China.[3] For Beijing, it is important to grasp opportunities to strengthen mutual interests. The report notes that there are "more points of agreement than divergences between the two parties, which should enable developing cooperation even more," adding that such strengthening is an integral part of the overall Chinese strategy. China's motivation is economic, although the Sino-European relationship is also sometimes seen by Beijing as a counterweight to the Sino-U.S. relationship,[4] which is much more competitive and challenging, as reflected in President Xi Jinping's visit to Washington in September 2015. (The topics discussed during the visit included cybersecurity, operations in the South China Sea, and the Chinese draft regulation on foreign nongovernmental organizations.) China's goal in preparing the April 2014 document was clearly to lay the groundwork for a free trade agreement. But while Brussels has been avoiding direct talks on such a treaty, Beijing seems for once to be making some concessions, as a condition for moving toward more technology transfers and gaining greater access to European markets: "We have the ability to sell not just toys, clothing, and shoes," Premier Li Keqiang said in March 2014, adding, "When the present parties respect each other and trade in a constructive manner, there is no reason not to work together."[5]

When Jean-Claude Juncker, former prime minister of Luxembourg, became president of the European Commission at the end of 2014, Sino-European relations took a turn for the better. The years 2010–14 had been marred by commercial disputes, starting with one over solar panels, followed by another over telecommunications. For the latter sector, it was the European trade commissioner Karel De Gucht who led the anti-Chinese revolt, softening his tone just a few days before he left office in October 2014. He denounced the disproportionate and unequal aid from Chinese banks (all state-owned) to the Chinese telecom equipment manufacturers Huawei and ZTE, which were accused of selling in foreign markets at less than the cost of production. (It should be noted that their prices were 18 percent lower than those of European manufacturers.) Between 2006 and 2014, Huawei's share of the European market went from 2.5 percent to 25 percent, a spectacular rise that was possible only thanks to aid from the Chinese state, as was explained in a working document prepared by the European Commission.[6] As for the dumping charge, Brussels and Beijing also reached an agreement to set a minimum sales price for solar panels. Finally, as a by-product of President Xi Jinping's historic visit to Brussels in the spring of 2014, the European Commission abandoned various criticisms—though not all approved of its moderating view. "I think that raising these irritating subjects will ultimately reinforce EU-China relations," Karel De Gucht concluded somewhat regretfully.[7] Efforts to make Beijing fall in line were hardly conclusive, however: in bilateral trade exchanges, the trade deficit rose to €137.8 billion in favor of China, which was far from the top supplier to the EU in 2014.

Another problem is that many foreign companies have been finding China increasingly difficult as a place to do business. For almost a decade, the European business community, represented by the EU Chamber of Commerce in China, has been complaining about market access in China. Each year, the Eurochamber publishes an incendiary report stressing the disequilibrium in market access at the expense of European enterprises in China, which suffer from "disproportionately restrictive rules."[8] The Eurochamber has called for a "significant retreat of political pressure from the business world in China." Bemoaned former chamber president David Cucino, "There is a very ideological point of view in China that considers we should be treated under a different regime because we are foreign enterprises." A recognized lobbyist, the Eurochamber stresses that many foreign firms are being scrutinized carefully, especially within the framework of China's anticorruption campaign. This is the case, for example, in the pharmaceuticals sector, where the Chinese government aggressively investigated and ultimately convicted GlaxoSmithKline of corruption and bribery of Chinese citizens, and in the agricultural and food sector, where food and dairy company Danone sustained a similar probe. Although China seeks to negotiate a Comprehensive Agreement on Investment (CAI) with the EU,[9] "it does not want this to be integrated into the notion of access to the market," wrote François Godement and Angela Stanzel in a policy brief.[10] On the other hand, rarely has China engaged so explicitly in collaboration with a group of nation-states. China is clearly seeking to formalize a bilateral investment treaty with the EU so as not to remain outside the major transatlantic (TTIP) and transpacific (TPP) negotiations. "The investment treaty is like a WTO for us, a rare opportunity for the EU to negotiate for more market access in times when Chinese companies seek a strong investment agreement in the EU," said Joerg Wuttke, the current Eurochamber president.[11]

HOW CHINA MAKES ITS VOICE HEARD IN BRUSSELS

Without any doubt, China's public relations effort has been professionalized. A senior Chinese diplomat in 2008, while part of the Chinese representation to the EU, told the authors in an interview that his work consisted of removing the landmines of "anti-Chinese campaigns" launched by the European Commission, the European Parliament, national delegations, and assorted pressure groups.[12] Unlike his colleagues' experience in European capitals, there were no cocktail parties and society functions for this diplomat, only serious and complex working meetings in the offices of the European Commission. Today the Chinese economic mission has provided itself with specialists in each technical domain, just as the other embassies in Brussels have. The Chinese press is also well represented in the Xinhua News Agency, CCTV, the *People's Daily*, and most of the other major newspapers. The correspondents of these media, who are more like "representatives," or lobbyists, participate actively in multiple round tables in Brussels on the future of China-EU relations (though such gatherings are often superficial).

More novel is the direct lobbying of the European institutions. Serge Abou is the former EU ambassador to China. In 2014 he unashamedly signed up as a senior adviser—that is, lobbyist—for the opaque Huawei Group to the European institutions. Nobody at the European Commission seems to take offense at the mixing of roles, though it is counter to European interests. Huawei, which spends upward of €3 million on lobbying, has recruited no fewer than seven public affairs officers for its European office, five lobbying agencies, and many outside consultants. This makes the telecommunication group, known for employing numerous European and American "advisers," the eighth largest group in terms of spending on Brussels lobbying, according to the European Parliament's Transparency Register.

Other Chinese companies are represented in Brussels, discreetly, and many Chinese professional groups pass through the offices of the European Commission and the European Parliament. For François Godement, a longtime expert on Sino-EU relations and the author of several studies on the subject, the EU's strategy in China has been based on an anachronistic belief, namely, that "China, under the influence of European involvement, was going to liberalize its economy, improve the rule of law, and to democratize,"[13] words that were heard equally often in the United States over the past several decades. But something else happened.

RELATIONS WITH FRANCE AND GERMANY: TEARING DOWN STEREOTYPES

The establishment of diplomatic relations with the PRC by President Charles de Gaulle on January 27, 1964, gave major French enterprises a place in the sun as early as the 1980s, in the framework of the Open Door policy under Deng Xiaoping, who returned to power at the end of 1978. Aided by numerous ministerial visits, the Franco-Chinese dialogue rapidly took the form of delegations of public or private investors, who benefited from formal credits in areas as varied as energy (Lyonnaise des Eaux, Framatome), urban transport (Alstom), telecommunications (Alcatel), and automobiles (Peugeot Citroën), resulting in "state-to-state" contracts. These contracts were often guaranteed by formal credits, such as those from Coface, for groups that did not really need them but benefited from the Jacobin generosity of a state concerned to appear in the foreground on the Beijing stage. It was a practice appreciated by China at the time. Certain paneuropean industrial groups knew in the 1980s and 1990s how to use the funds of various European governments (Italy, the Netherlands, Germany, Belgium, Spain) to advance their own investments at a time when China had great need of infrastructure. The French global communications company Alcatel, for example, between 1990 and 2000 counted a dozen subsidiaries in China, all of different nationalities.

Beginning with Valéry Giscard d'Estaing, who made the trip in 1980, all French presidents have visited China, the high point of such relations being the visit of Jacques Chirac, who opened wide the doors of the republic's palaces to official Chinese visitors. But such efforts did not necessarily produce a harvest in trade: on the contrary, the Franco-Chinese commercial deficit was dug in the years 1995–2007. Successive French governments often served as mediators in dealing with the Chinese authorities on behalf of their European colleagues, in particular the Benelux countries and the Federal Republic of Germany, before the latter established its own embassy, which was later merged with the embassy of the former German Democratic Republic in Beijing in 1990. The Chinese strategy of the European Commission, described above, actually began in 1985, and was partly inspired by French advice, in which the interests of the CAC 40 (the French stock market index of the forty largest companies) and the state were combined.

In 2015 the spirit changed. For the previous thirty years China had enjoyed stunning economic growth. Having long been the factory to the developed world's multinationals, the country began to acquire leading corporations in technology and industry, whose products then landed on Western markets. Inspired by Germany, the appliance manufacturer Haier, headquartered in the city of Qingdao, became the world's leading producer of refrigerators: in 2013, after making several acquisitions, its sales figures reached $26 billion. Lenovo, after acquiring the personal computer division of IBM in 2004, announced in 2014 that it had bought from the same American group its System X division for $2.5 billion, thus attracting to its camp another 7,500 engineers. Of note, this stalwart has won several foreign state contracts, including an unconfirmed computing contract worth €160 million from the French Ministry of Defense, which is surprising, since the agreement concerns storing and safeguarding confidential data.

As the world's second strongest commercial power, China today wants "win-win" partnerships, and the contribution of credits no longer suffices, as demonstrated by the presence of an Airbus factory in Tianjin (an investment of $645 million), which will develop from 2016 the A320neo version; among its competitors are a Chinese-built 100-seat aircraft, the C919, whose design and construction are supplied by a Chinese group from Shanghai (COMAC) in alliance with the French defense firm Safran. Similarly, the Franco-Chinese civil nuclear project is promising: a 2011 accord between Electricité de France (EDF) and the China National Nuclear Corporation will permit, through a transfer of technology (and Chinese funding), joint development of the civil nuclear market, especially in the United Kingdom and perhaps later in South Africa.

Now the partners have to find new ideas, since the French government has no more formal credits or a magic wand. Of course, there are many kinds of cooperation in educational and cultural spheres, but the Chinese public seems to have been seduced more by the sirens of Hollywood than by French artists. On the economic level, certain French industrial groups with a long presence in the country have succeeded in building a solid relationship with China, but the door to public markets is often closed to them. China wants more technology transfers, hence the relative success of Germany, its major European partner, which in the early 1980s has not hesitated to commit to a long-term business relationship.

In Chinese eyes, France does not have the image of an industrial and technological country. On the other hand, it has known brands, and French products related to the "art of living" are recognized in China for their quality. The same is true of agro-food and health, sectors in which the Chinese middle classes are no longer satisfied with local offerings. Powdered milk is routinely imported by China, for example. Generally speaking, French SMBs—small and medium-sized businesses—have a weak presence in the Chinese market since they are less accustomed to exporting than their German neighbors. Of course, there are a few alliances, such as the rapprochement in 2008 between a Shandong firm, Weichai, and the Baudouin motor manufacturer in Cassis, but that remains an isolated case, and profits are not yet forthcoming.

No doubt the centralized French state system is partly responsible for this situation. The efforts of local communities are recent, insufficient, and fragmentary. Conversely, the image of China in France is also divorced from reality and is often a caricature. With respect to education, twenty years ago there were only a few hundred Chinese students studying in France, while today there are nearly 50,000, with the numbers increasing by 10 percent per year.[14] This is a real success, if belated, and here again, Anglo-American power dominates (274,000 Chinese students were studying in the United States in 2014, out of a total of 886,052 studying abroad, according to the Institute of International Education).[15] But France could construct a veritable network of friendships through its brands, its leading products, its universities, its museums, and even its SMBs, so why forgo the opportunity? For that to happen, however, French society must take the measure of the stakes involved and send more trainees, interns, students, and scholars to China as a way of undertaking direct actions to build solid ties with Chinese society, without the government necessarily intervening.

President Xi Jinping's state visit to France in March 2014 still stands as the pinnacle of those sumptuous events that only the Republic of France can stage-manage, entailing a state dinner at the Élysée Palace, a concert at Versailles, and high-level conferences at Bercy and at the Quai d'Orsay.[16] But in the end, few contracts were signed. One was the highly touted purchase of a 14 percent share in the capital of the French car firm PSA Peugeot-Citroën by the Chinese group Dongfeng for the sum of €800 million; another was the purchase (in return for technology transfers) of a thousand Airbus EC175 helicopters for $8 billion. These helicopters will be constructed jointly with the Chinese aeronautic giant AVIC, through a technology transfer. And earlier, the China Investment Corporation, the country's top sovereign wealth fund, had taken a 30 percent stake in the capital of GDF Suez Exploration (now part of Engie) with the aid of the French state credit bank Caisse des Dépôts et Consignations. After the renewal of friendship following the difficult years of 2008–11, a new key concern has appeared: how to get French and Chinese civil societies, which still appear quite remote from each other, to work together.

On the ground, several investment projects remain uncertain. In the Normandy port of Le Havre, Hsueh Sheng Wang, a Franco-Chinese businessman from Wenzhou and president of Eurasia, an obscure SMB (turnover of $18 million), declared in 2011 that he wanted to invest $22 million in a port multimodal warehouse project that was supposed to create 700 local jobs. He had promised to bring more Chinese investors and to establish a hub in Le Havre. But the results were delayed, and the mayor's office became impatient.[17] "It is nothing more than a warehouse," moaned Mayor Edouard Philippe in July 2013.[18] As another example, the Shenzhen-based network company and smartphone manufacturer ZTE, courted and granted special concessions by France, frequently announced extremely lucrative investments from its French headquarters, near the science-themed Futuroscope amusement park in Poitiers, but results were not forthcoming, and most of the costly headquarters building no longer houses ZTE. It seems the Chinese company and the French authorities were never able to agree on the actual business activities to take place in the ZTE Poitiers facilities. (A local Confucius Institute, by contrast, was created with the devoted assistance of the Chinese government.) Several other ambitious real estate deals are in gestation, including Terra Lorraine, managed by the regional council of Lorraine in eastern France, which is meant to attract hundreds of Chinese enterprises, and the Châteauroux Business District, promised to the city of Châteauroux by a big Chinese investor, Beijing Capital Land. The Bank of China is covering the risk, which is not small. As suggested by these several cases of predominantly real estate ventures, results have been mixed, but generally less than what either France had hoped for or China had promoted.

Another fruitful sector is food processing, especially with investment from the Synutra group in Carhaix, Brittany. In 2011 Jean-Yves Le Drian, member of the French Socialist Party and president of the Brittany region, received a Chinese delegation from Shandong province. As recounted by Richard Ferrand, a Socialist Member of Parliament from Finistère: "The Chinese told us that in their country there was no milk production and Chinese families were worried, particularly about powdered milk for newborn children. . . . So France represented high food quality to them."[19] After many vicissitudes (owing principally to the slowness of the Chinese and French bureaucracies), the Synutra group decided to invest €100 million in a dairy factory in Carhaix in Finistère. This huge factory, still under construction, is expected to open this year. But local people are not so sure how many business opportunities will arise for Finisterian agriculture. Moreover, the year 2013 saw the opening of the Chinese market to a French pig subsidiary, as well as permission for a dozen French producers to export their products to the Chinese market. Chinese inspectors did a tour in 2014, shortly before the first exports were expected. As of this writing, exports have barely started moving.

During this time, Germany was multiplying its own initiatives, benefiting from an extremely favorable context. China has long believed in an enlarged Europe (especially after the integration of ten new countries into the EU in 2004), and Germany is now its priority in Europe. For many years, the heart of China's power structure has been its engineers, often graduates of the best engineering schools in the country (such as Tsinghua, Tongji, and Jiaotong), who look favorably on German industry. Germany's manufacturing excellence has been recognized in China since the end of the 1980s, when Chinese entrepreneurs, especially in the Special Economic Zones of Shenzhen and Xiamen, boasted about their brand-new and technically flawless German machinery.

The Chinese fascination with German engineering was evident at the 2010 Shanghai World Expo. The German pavilion, situated alongside the French one, attracted fewer Chinese visitors than its neighbor, but Chinese citizens interested in science stayed longer and were clearly keen on the appliances, which had been installed in a visually arresting way, whereas France presented itself as a leader of the fashion and luxury industries. "Generally speaking, Germans appear more open to Chinese entrepreneurs, they focus on the long term, and their system is simpler than the French, who are perceived as overly ideological," remarked Meng Fanchen, a former executive of Siemens China who has lived and worked in both Germany and France.[20]

To understand the importance of Germany to the Chinese economy, it is enough to observe the German Internet sites extolling "German power" to Chinese investors.[21] This message is echoed in China, to which German exports rose from 1 percent of the country's total exports in 2000 to 6.5 percent in 2013. Almost half the European exports to China are German. The reelection of Chancellor Angela Merkel in September 2013 only strengthened China's desire to cooperate with the major European power, with some even referring to a "special partnership" between the two countries. And despite the revived relations between China and France in 2014, capped by the state visit by President Xi Jinping, the rapprochement with Germany has become political. Angela Merkel travels to China almost once a year. During her last (and eighth) visit, in November 2015, she reportedly raised difficult points, including market access, cybersecurity issues, and intellectual property rights, but also the proposed draft of a new Chinese law on foreign nongovernmental organizations and human rights issues. Traveling with her, as it is often the case, were twenty German CEOs. Between the chancellor's visits, numerous trips by cabinet ministers and minister-presidents of the länder, the sixteen federal states of Germany, also take place.

The China Investment Corporation and state-owned enterprises (SOEs) have been encouraged to seek opportunities in Germany, where industrialists have enjoyed long-standing relations with the Chinese market, for example in the automobile sector. Volkswagen has been installed in Shanghai since 1985 and for thirty years has supplied the taxi companies with their leading model, the locally manufactured Santana. (The Santana was originally made in collaboration with the Shanghai Tractor Automobile Corporation, which evolved into the SAIC Group.) This vehicle is legendary. In 1984 Volkswagen, along with the China National Automotive Industry Corporation and the Bank of China, signed a contract with Shanghai Tractor Automobile Corporation that led to the formation of the joint venture Shanghai Volkswagen Automotive. Beginning in 1982 with a few hundred vehicles rolling off the assembly line, Santana ended up producing 3.2 million vehicles before this model was discontinued in 2013. But the adventure in China continued for Volkswagen,[22] as it has for the other German car manufacturers that have made China their priority: all have agreed to invest in the various regions suggested by the Chinese government. Other German sectors of high interest to China for investment include renewable energy, high technology, and machine tools.

Significant German investments in China as well as trade exchanges are now accompanied by Chinese investments in Germany, although the proportions remain lopsided: €45 billion of German investment in China, versus €6.9 billion of Chinese investment in Germany. Germany is now the second largest recipient of Chinese overseas direct investment in Europe, according to a recent report by the Mercator Institute for China Studies.[23]

But as confirmed by Chancellor Merkel's trip to China and by President Xi Jinping's visit to Germany in April 2014, the Sino-German partnership is solid. During Xi's trip there were no shows of splendor or private concerts; instead, Xi was taken to visit North Rhine–Westphalia, one of the most industrial länder in the country. No fewer than twenty-five German industrial enterprises were acquired by China during 2013, three times more than in 2010. "The two most important sectors are automotive and industrial equipment with €1.9 billion and €2.7 billion of investment deals respectively, reflecting great Chinese interest in high-end manufacturing assets," the Mercator Institute report stated.[24] And according to several studies, this trend is expected to continue to 2020. Of course, the investments include some older SOEs from the former East Germany, but the majority are SMBs controlled by family capital in the old states of the former West Germany.

One of the best examples of this arrival of Chinese capital in Germany is the purchase at the start of 2012 of the family machine tool business Putzmeister (3,000 employees) by the state-owned Chinese company Sany Heavy Industry (70,000 employees). This was a €360 million investment. The founder of Putzmeister, aged seventy-nine, did not find heirs capable of carrying the torch and so welcomed a Sany that had just finished the construction of a brand-new research and development center for more than €100 million. The purchase of Putzmeister was a shock to the German business culture, as well as representing a "clash of civilizations," in the words of Samuel Huntington.[25] Putzmeister Holding is a manufacturer of machines for the construction industry, in particular concrete pumps used in buildings and mines and in the construction of tunnels for major industrial projects. This partnering of two industrial giants, one Chinese, one German, is historic.

The two partners say they are profiting from a new constellation. The financial solidity of Sany securitizes the growth prospects of Putzmeister and gives the company a considerable advantage over the competition. Meanwhile, Sany has completed its portfolio with state-of-the-art technologies and German-made innovations, and has acquired a solid network for distribution and services outside China. On the ground at Aichtal, the employees are somewhat perplexed about the management methods of the new bosses. "It took a good two years for the engineers of Putzmeister to accept taking orders from the Chinese," explains a consultant charged with supervising the transition.[26] But now profits have started to come in. Sany will pursue its European breakthrough with the purchase of a second German firm, Intermix, and with the creation of a joint venture with the Austrian group Palfinger.

The 2012 acquisition of a small family business (1,000 employ-ees), the German computer seller Medion, by China's Lenovo also bears mentioning. The deal was effectively conducted by group CEO Yang Yanqing himself. "At first we asked questions about the inte-gration of this new subsidiary, but the Chinese are fascinated by Germany," said a Lenovo European executive.[27] The acquisition of Medion has enabled Lenovo to develop activities aimed at the gen-eral public in Germany, and to learn "the German method." This acquisition was held up as an example to all the countries of Europe, and even to the United States (site of the former IBM divisions that became Lenovo) and China. Today, Lenovo is the largest maker of personal computers in Germany, proof of a successful graft, accord-ing to Gianfranco Lanci, former president of Lenovo in Europe and now global COO of the corporation. "We are a Chinese *and* global group, that is most important."[28]

There is one cloud over the scene, though: a reduction in Ger-man investments in China, in particular by Siemens. "The retreat of the major German groups in China might feed an anti-Chinese sentiment," notes Michael Schaefer, who was the German ambas-sador to Beijing from 2007 to 2013.[29] Like their Western counter-parts, German industrialists face increasingly restricted access to the Chinese market, and some have begun to withdraw, which might imperil the balance of Sino-German economic relations. Moreover, the tightening of credit in China means that six-month delays in payment are more difficult to manage for German firms, which also suffer from increasingly effective Chinese competition.

CHINA NIBBLES AT ITALY, GREECE, PORTUGAL, AND SPAIN

In June 2014, Li Keqiang spent three days in Greece—an excep-tional duration for an official trip—which led to no less than nine-teen cooperation agreements and commercial contracts, for a total amount of €3.4 billion. Shortly afterward, Xi Jinping himself made a stopover in Greece, where he was welcomed with fanfare by the Greek president and prime minister.

The principal victim of the financial crisis that struck Europe after 2007, Greece scarcely hesitated to call on Chinese capital to fill its coffers, largely encouraged in this by the lenders—the European Commission, the European Central Bank, and the International Monetary Fund (IMF). In 2008, the concession given to COSCO (Chinese Overseas Shipping Group Co.), the Chinese state-owned giant in marine transport, for the management of two terminals in Athens's Port of Piraeus, for the sum of €500 million and a lease period of thirty years, constituted one of the most visible actions by China. The concession was later extended for another five years. The investment now ranks as one of the most successful Greek privatizations in recent decades. For the past six years, COSCO has successfully upgraded the infrastructure, introduced more efficient machinery and equipment, dealt with the labor unions,[30] improved the management system, and created more traffic in the port. In 2008, the year before COSCO came to town, Piraeus moved just 433,582 containers. In 2014, that number grew more than seven-fold, to 3.16 million containers—and 80 percent of that growth has been attributed to COSCO, which runs Piers II and III and employs 1,200 workers, whereas the Greek state-owned OLP Port Authority runs Pier I and employs 800 workers.[31] Moreover, the use of Athens as a logistical base opens up new possibilities for Chinese indus-trialists to send their products by train to Central Europe and the Balkans.

In 2013, COSCO chose to increase its investments by renovating—for €230 million—the existing terminals, thus making Piraeus its port of entry into Europe. There was talk of 400 jobs created and of a possible total privatization of the port.

Meanwhile, COSCO has further plans to expand, moves that the company expects will boost volumes to more than 6 million con-tainers by 2016. The Chinese port operator has installed eleven new loading cranes, which should put its Piraeus operations roughly on equal footing with capacity at Rotterdam, Antwerp, and Hamburg, Europe's three busiest container ports.

Also being studied was participation in the capital of the port authority, and even the purchase of the Ellinikon airport south of Athens to create a leisure complex in the mode of Dubai. China said at the time it was also interested in constructing an airport at Kasteli and a port at Thymbaki, both on Crete. Ultimately, China wants to use Athens as a hub for operations in the Balkans and the Mediterranean Sea. The success of the Greek far left party, Syriza, in the elections of January 2015, however, put a brake on the privatization of the port of Athens, and on several other Chinese projects in Greece as well. Although the former Greek finance minister, Yanis Varoufakis, estimated during a visit to Washington that "this problem will be solved,"[32] it seems the Chinese government did not appreciate the backpedaling and speculated about the risks to its investments resulting from democratic elections in Europe. But since September 2015, a reelected Alexis Tsipras has sent signals that his government still wants to privatize the majority of the Piraeus Port Authority in the not so distant future. China COSCO Holdings Co. is now the sole bidder for Piraeus. As several big Chinese companies (ZTE, Huawei) have started moving part of their European operations to the Athens harbor, China's hub expansion might just be around the corner.

Milan is the economic and financial capital of Italy, so it is no surprise that the founders of Mandarin Capital Partners elected to settle there. At the headquarters of this group, situated in the heart of Milan, a visitor is welcomed with good-quality tea from Hunan province. The timing was good, since Mandarin Capital accomplished one of the best Sino-European operations of recent years through the acquisition of CIFA (Compagnia Italiana Forme Acciaio, a machine tools manufacturer) by its rival but also business partner, Zoomlion Heavy Industry, a deal that was concluded in August 2013 for €500 million. In 2011, CIFA was on the verge of bankruptcy, and because the family that owned it was divided, it did not get the support of creditors. The operation permitted CIFA to construct, with its new shareholder, a new factory in Changsha, the capital of Hunan province, and to integrate some of its R&D teams. "Zhan Chunxin, president of Zoomlion, is a particularly open Chinese entrepreneur, and he trusted us," said Lorenzo Stanca, managing partner of Mandarin Capital Partners, which served as the intermediary with Milanese business circles.[33] Moreover, the Italian boss of CIFA has become vice-chairman of the new group, Zoomlion CIFA (H.K.) Holdings Co.

In Tuscany, the small town of Prato, some 300 kilometers from Milan, hosts a Chinese population of almost 50,000, or a quarter of the inhabitants of Prato. Most come from Wenzhou, the coastal town in Zhejiang from which a majority of the Chinese in Europe come. Artisans, traders, small industrialists, real estate promoters, and software designers, they speak a dialect that differentiates them from other Chinese, and their relations with compatriots from the north of China are often complex. For twenty-some years the Italian government has left this community to develop on its own, despite the obvious presence of a significant number of illegal immigrants. This "Chinatown" has become a veritable training center for Chinese entrepreneurs in Europe. Those who settled twenty years ago teach new arrivals about local customs. The sectors that interest Chinese entrepreneurs in the rest of Italy include fashion, automobiles, food processing, machine tools, and, of course, telecommunications (Huawei has opened an R&D center near Milan for its mass-market products), and even e-commerce, which pushed the IZP Technologies Group to open offices there in 2013. China's State Grid Corporation thus acquired 35 percent of CDP Reti, the Italian national gas and electricity agency. The luxury yacht manufacturer Ferretti has also passed into the hands of Chinese investors, as has the Parma airport, bought for €200 million by IZP Technologies (though the company had no prior experience in this domain). Moreover, the Chinese State Administration of Foreign

Exchange has bought Italian treasury bonds in euros and acquired participation in such companies as Eni and Enel (energy), Fiat Chrysler (automotive), Telecom Italia, and Ferragamo (clothing and shoes). According to a study by the *Financial Times,* 200 Italian SMBs have been bought by Chinese investors for a total of €6 billion.[34] The commercial deficit between Italy and China, it should be noted, currently stands at €15 billion, in favor of China. "China has one objective: infiltrate the block of Western countries and separate Europe from the United States; to do this the Chinese are beginning with the weakest countries like Italy," the economist Alberto Forchielli, cofounder of Mandarin Capital Partners, has said.[35] In this connection, the purchase of the tire giant Pirelli by the China National Chemical Corporation on March 22, 2015, for the sum of $7.7 billion marked a key moment in the history of Chinese investments in Italy. "From now on, Italian industrial policy is made in Beijing," the former Italian prime minister Romano Prodi is rumored to have said.[36]

In 2004, China signed strategic partnerships with four countries: Germany, France, the United Kingdom, and Portugal. With Germany, Beijing aimed at an economic partnership; with France, it sought a multilateral dialogue through the United Nations; and with Britain, it considered the financial stature of the City of London and sought to leverage long-standing relations formed around the former British colony of Hong Kong. Other considerations took into account the importance of the Commonwealth, the use of the English language globally, and multilateralism. But why did Portugal, whose tottering economy, like that of Greece, made life difficult in Brussels after the financial crisis of 2008?

There are many reasons. China recognizes the political weight of the former Portuguese empire through the spread of its language: there are more than 220 million Portuguese speakers in the world. In 1996, seven Portuguese-speaking countries created a new community, the Comunidade dos Países de Língua Portuguesa, based on their shared language. Apart from Brazil, Angola, and Mozambique (a country where China has many economic interests), of particular interest is the very special relation between the former Portuguese enclave of Macau, a peninsula north of Hong Kong, and the former Middle Kingdom, which retook possession of the territory in 1999 after more than four centuries of Portuguese colonization. Each year the Macau Forum celebrates—in the presence of a Chinese vice premier—the relationship between Beijing and Lisbon through Macau.

On the investment side, the Chinese of Hong Kong quickly steered for Lisbon in the late 1990s. Stanley Ho, the Portuguese-speaking king of the Macau casinos, started investing in Portuguese real estate even earlier. Today, agencies specializing in the provision of "golden visas" are increasing in Spain and Portugal.[37] The principle is simple: whoever invests a minimum of €500,000 in real estate property may obtain a long-stay visa; the minimal obligation is to spend seven days in the country. After six years, the investor can ask for Portuguese nationality, which allows him or her to obtain an EU passport. In Cyprus, the invested sum falls to €300,000, and in Greece it is only €250,000. Of course, this procedure still affects only some hundreds of persons (734 in Portugal), but it is expressly aimed at wealthy Chinese nationals who want to emigrate.[38] Up until now, the number of jobs created as a result of large external investments sufficient to acquire a visa has remained very small (and perhaps to be found chiefly in the real estate business), and the results are mixed, but several Chinese groups have made important investments, such as Fosun, which has invested €1 million to take 80 percent of the capital of Caixa Seguros, the insurance branch of the state bank Caixa Geral de Depósitos. This was not the first time that Lisbon chose a Chinese company, as these groups always made the best offer: in 2011 the Portuguese government sold 21.3 percent of the public electric company Energias de Portugal to China's state-owned power enterprise, Three Gorges Corporation, for €2.7 billion, preferring it to the offer from the Düsseldorf-based E·ON; it also sold

25 percent of the national grid management firm to benefit China's State Grid Corporation for €390 million.[39]

The situation of the former Spanish colonial empire has not yet pushed Spain into the arms of Chinese investors. For years, the Spanish presence in China was among the most minor, limited to only cultural and educational activities, some businesses, and the Spanish press. There are no more than 200,000 Chinese settled in Spain, including 8,000 students. Until now it has been the small business owners of Wenzhou and the neighboring city of Qingtian that made China known to the Spaniards—and not necessarily for the best.[40]

Margaret Hong Chen, a woman from Shanghai married to a Spaniard, settled in Madrid twenty-one years ago, worked for a long time at Telefónica, and created the company's subsidiary in Beijing. "To this day there has never been a Chinese person highly placed in this group, proof that the two cultures have a hard time understanding each other," she says.[41] As founding president of the China Club of Spain, which has 130 members, she tries to integrate Chinese executives working for major Spanish firms, as well as bankers, lawyers, and accountants, into the local economic network. This population perfectly complements the Chinese expatriates affiliated with various Chinese business networks, including the business school ESADE (Escuela Superior de Administración y Dirección de Empresas, part of Ramon Llull University) in Barcelona.

Spain may serve as a jumping-off point for Chinese groups targeting Latin America. In fact, China is already present there in force, and its entry into South America did not wait for Spanish help. Spain is perhaps realizing this, as are Chinese corporations such as ZTE or Huawei, which have installed their senior managers in charge of their Telefónica account in Spain but are also expanding their operations on the South American continent.

Meanwhile, after buying 48 percent of the French airline company Aigle Azur in 2012, the HNA Group, parent of China's Hainan

Airline Co., acquired 20 percent of the Spanish hotel chain NH Hoteles (expecting that tourism would become strategic in time). "They have gradually placed their own people in NH, including among the European board members," recounted a former senior executive in an interview.[42] Other recent acquisitions are the food-processing group Campofrio and Osborne beverages, as well as the well-publicized purchase of Edificio España, a well-known building in Madrid in the neobaroque style, bought for €265 million. Like Portugal, Spain offers a special residence permit to Chinese investors in real estate (for property worth more than €500,000) or in projects of general utility with job creation. At the end of ten years, the right of permanent residence in Spain is granted (in contrast to only five years in Greece and Portugal, as noted).

China does not neglect Eastern Europe, in particular the two countries that Chinese firms have been using as bases for subcontracting: Romania and Hungary. During the "16 + 1" summit held in Belgrade in December 2014, and in the presence of Li Keqiang and sixteen leaders of Central and Eastern European countries, the Chinese prime minister announced the establishment of a €3 billion fund designed to encourage Chinese investors to engage in public-private partnerships and in the privatization of certain enterprises in the Central and Eastern European zone. Similarly, Beijing has announced the financing of a new railroad between Belgrade and Budapest. Still wanting to advance its plan for a new Silk Road, China continues to closely examine certain port and airport infrastructures in Bulgaria, Slovenia, and Croatia. These countries may offer excellent points of entry into the euro zone, with the cheapest production costs. The fourth "16 + 1" meeting took place in November 2015 in the Chinese city of Suzhou. In an interview with the authors shortly afterward, a senior official of the Chinese Ministry of Foreign Affairs explained that the group had made "great progress," including the signing of seven bilateral agreements in the form of MoUs (memoranda of understanding) in relation to the "One Belt, One Road" initiative.[43]

THE PASSION FOR THE UNITED KINGDOM

On the other side of the English Channel, the Chinese are aiming not at access to the European market but rather at the international financial center of London, which in 2015, during President Xi Jinping's state visit, was officially described as the first official international platform for renminbi currency trading.[44] According to the City of London, London markets hosted $61.5 billion worth of renminbi trading per day in 2014, up 143 percent on 2013 levels.

But it is not just about finance: Since 2012 the Chinese have invested (or signed promises to invest) more than €10 billion, as much as it had over the previous thirty years. After a rather turbulent shared history, dating from the Opium Wars in the mid-1800s and the colonization of Hong Kong, which lasted until 1997, the United Kingdom suddenly became the preferred destination for Chinese investors (see table 1-1).

The favorite sectors for investment are real estate and infrastructure, but finance, new technologies, and higher education are also strong (in 2014 there were 88,000 Chinese students, including 38,000 undergraduates, studying in the United Kingdom). In London, one major transaction relating to the acquisition of commercial and residential buildings has been signed each trimester, to the regret of Paris and Frankfurt, which lost that potential investment. From participation in two major airports to a high-speed train line, via electricity stations, China has lavished hundreds of thousands of euros on the British Isles, with a preference for London. The City of London in turn has signed an unprecedented agreement authorizing the largest private bank in China, the China Minsheng Bank, to establish its European headquarters there and has given the green light to the China Merchant Bank, the third largest Chinese brokerage house, to establish its first trading platform in Europe. China has acquired brands like Weetabix and Pizza Express, it has invested in the airports of Heathrow and Manchester, and it will invest— alongside the French, which is doubly astonishing—in the future

TABLE I-I. *Chinese FDI in All Twenty-Eight EU Countries, 2000–14*

COUNTRY	TOTAL FDI AMOUNT (MILLIONS OF USD)
1. United Kingdom	16,000
2. Germany	8,400
3. France	8,000
4. Portugal	6,700
5. Italy	5,600
6. Belgium, Hungary, the Netherlands, Spain, Sweden (each)	1,000–5,000
7. Austria, Greece, Luxembourg, Poland, Romania (each)	500–1,000
8. Bulgaria, Czech Republic, Denmark, Finland, Ireland (each)	100–500
9. Croatia, Cyprus, Estonia, Latvia, Lithuania, Malta, Slovakia, Slovenia (each)	>100

SOURCE: *Rhodium Group/Baker & McKenzie, "Reaching New Heights: An Update on Chinese Investments in Europe," 2015.*

nuclear power station of Hinkley Point C. This Franco-Chinese project (led by Electricité de France) has received the approval of the British authorities and will be jointly financed by the China National Nuclear Corporation, the China General Nuclear Power Group, and France. As for Huawei, it has promised to invest £1.2 billion in the United Kingdom,[45] and, always concerned with its image, Huawei has just signed a two-year sponsoring contract with the famous Arsenal football club—nothing sells better in a country passionate about soccer.

What accounts for this fascination with Britain when until recently Germany seemed the preferred target of the Chinese? The British superiority in finance, real estate, and higher education is recognized worldwide, placing the United Kingdom just behind the United States in attractiveness to investors: the English language, the size and liquidity of markets, a high reputation, the potential for profit in capital, and a fiscal system comprehensible to philistines are all comparative advantages in relation to neighboring and competing countries such as France, Benelux, and Germany.

British "pragmatism" (a word often repeated and praised by Chinese officials in conversations) and voluntarism also count for a lot, with the United Kingdom seeking to strengthen as well as to normalize, as much as possible, its relations with China and to avoid provocative subjects. Three great events have shaped this ambition: the official visit by David Cameron in December 2013, accompanied by a plethora of ministers and business leaders, followed six months later by a return visit in great pomp by Premier Li Keqiang, who was granted the signal honor of meeting the Queen, and subsequently an even grander state visit by Xi Jinping on October 20, 2015. The Chinese president and his wife, the soprano Peng Liyuan, were hosted by the Queen at Buckingham Palace and rode in a royal carriage, and Xi addressed both houses of the British Parliament. But official visits are not just about protocol and glamour. Rather, such encounters are the result of negotiations relating to the entry of the Chinese into infrastructure projects, through public-private partnerships that are generally closed to third-party countries or to nations that are reputed to be unreliable. Nothing of the kind occurs in the United Kingdom, where the lure of gain seems to dominate. David Cameron himself explained that he "had no difficulty with the fact that China is investing in nuclear power, in airports, and even in infrastructure linked to water."[46] Chinese sovereign funds took 9 percent of the capital of Thames Water, the principal water treatment company in Britain. Other investments (some still unconfirmed) include a high-speed train between London and Manchester, the massive development of a "northern power house" in northern England, and other energy or infrastructure projects. But the majority of Chinese investments remain property-related, both office and residential. To the other inducements should then be added a costly program of access to resident status: an investment

TABLE 1-2. *Top Twenty-One China-EU Deals in 2014–15*

TARGET	COUNTRY	ACQUIRER	SECTOR	VALUE (MILLIONS OF USD)	SHARE (%)	YEAR
1. Pirelli	Italy	ChemChina	Auto industry	7,700	100	2015
2. CDP Reti	Italy	State Grid Corporation of China	Energy	2,600	35	2014
3. Vivat	Netherlands	Anbang Insurance Group	Finance	1,870	100	2015
4. Pizza Express	United Kingdom	Hony	Agriculture and food	1,540	100	2014
5. Royal Albert Docks (Asian business port)	United Kingdom	Minsheng Investment	Real estate	1,500	N/A	2015
6. Groupe du Louvre	France	Jin Jiang International Holdings	Real estate	1,490	100	2014
7. Eight French shopping centers, including La Vache Noire, and two Belgian shopping centers	France and Belgium	China Investment Corp.	Real estate	1,430	N/A	2015
8. Canary Wharf	United Kingdom	China Life Insurance Co.	Real estate	1,400	70	2014
9. Caixa Seguros e Saúde	Portugal	Fosun	Insurance	1,360	80	2014
10. 10 Upper Bank Street (office building)	United Kingdom	China Life Insurance	Real estate	1,350	N/A	2014

11. Chiswick Park	United Kingdom	China Investment Corporation	Real estate	1,300	N/A	2014
12. Nidera	Netherlands	COFCO	Agriculture and food	1,290	51	2014
13. Club Med	France	Fosun	Entertainment and hospitality	1,120	97	2015
14. Peugeot	France	Dongfeng	Auto industry	1,100	28	2014
15. Highland Group Holdings Ltd. (House of Fraser)	United Kingdom	Nanjing Xinjiekou Department Store	Consumer products and services	790	N/A	2014
16. Hilite	Germany	AVIC	Automotive and transport equipment	644	19.03[a]	2014
17. Espirito Santo Saúde	Portugal	Fosun	Health care and biotechnology	590	51	2014
18. Ansaldo Energia	Italy	Shanghai Electric	Industrial equipment	557	N/A	2014
19. Salov	Italy	Bright Food	Agriculture and food	390	N/A	2014
20. Edificio España	Spain	Dalian Wanda Group	Real estate	358	N/A	2014
21. Carmelite Riverside	United Kingdom	China Overseas Holdings Ltd.	Real estate	280	N/A	2014

SOURCES: *BBC*, *Bloomberg*, Wall Street Journal, New York Times, China Daily, *Forbes*, *Reuters*, Financial Times, Telegraph (*UK*), Guardian (*UK*), FinanceAsia.

a. AIVC already owns 20 percent of Hilite.

TABLE 1-3. *Top Twenty China-EU Deals in 2008–14*

TARGET	COUNTRY	ACQUIRER	SECTOR	VALUE (MILLIONS OF USD)	SHARE (%)	YEAR
1. Rio Tinto PLC	United Kingdom	Aluminum Corp of China (Alcoa)	Basic materials	14,135		2008
2. Eni Spa	Italy	China National Petroleum Corp	Energy	4,210		2013
3. Energias de Portugal SA	Portugal	China Three Gorges Corp	Energy	3,510		2011
4. GDF Suez Exploration	France	China Investment Corp.	Financial	3,264		2011
5. Barclays PLC	United Kingdom	China Development Bank Corp., China General Nuclear Power Holding Corp.	Financial	3,062	3	2007
6. Volvo Personvagnar AB	Sweden	Zhejiang Geely Holding Group	Consumer	1,800		2010
7. Borsod Chem Zrt	Hungary	Wanhua Industrial Group	Basic materials	1,552		2011
8. Talisman Sinopec Energy UK	United Kingdom	China Petroleum & Chemical Corp	Energy	1,500		2012
9. InterGen NV	Netherlands	China Huaneng Group Corp	Utilities	1,232		2010

No.	Company	Country	Chinese Investor	Sector	Value	Stake %	Year
10.	Weetabix	United Kingdom	Bright Food Group	Consumer	1,165		2012
11.	KION Group AG	Germany	Weichai Power Co.	Industrials	1,136		2012
12.	Ineos	United Kingdom	PetroChina Co.	Energy	1,015		2011
13.	Apax Partners LLP	United Kingdom	China Investment Corp.	Financial	956	2	2010
14.	Kalahari Minerals	United Kingdom	China Development Bank Corp., China General Nuclear Power Holding Corp.	Basic materials	935		2011
15.	UPP Group Holdings	United Kingdom	Gingko Tree Investment	Financial	869		2013
16.	CLSA BV	Netherlands	CITIC Securities	Financial	842		2012
17.	Emerald Energy PLC	United Kingdom	Sinochem Group	Basic materials	736	100	2009
18.	FGP TopCo	United Kingdom	China Investment Corp.	Financial	726		2012
19.	Putzmeister Holding	Germany	Sany Heavy Industry Co.	Industrials	689		2012
20.	Redes Energeticas Nacionais	Portugal	China State Grid Corporation	Utilities	509		2012

SOURCE: *Deutsche Bank Research, China-EU Relations: Gearing up for Growth, July 21, 2014.*

NOTES: *Table includes complete M&A, investment, and joint ventures where value is disclosed on Bloomberg. Listings are as of January to May, 2014.*

of at least £2 million wins a promise of permanent residency after five years.

The desire to attract Chinese investors is found at all administrative levels, starting with Chancellor of the Exchequer George Osborne, who made the decision, much to the chagrin of the White House,[47] to join the Asian Infrastructure Investment Bank, launched by Beijing. The main British business body, the U.K.-China Business Council, has an efficient team that is dispatched to Beijing and several other Chinese cities. In London, it organizes numerous events on China, hoping to attract investors but also to help British companies in China. Many local British authorities, starting with London (London and Partners), have offices specifically dedicated to welcoming Chinese investors and deploying vast sums to seduce this clientele. Andrew Finney, the deputy mayor of Basingstoke in charge of economic affairs, who has often assisted the inevitable Huawei in its attempts to open facilities in his town, situated between London and Southampton, has expressed the ambient philosophy: "Our approach is pragmatic and oriented to the client, whatever his origin or past. Gone is the bureaucracy and its procedures; we act as managers without qualms."[48] Despite all this support, the intentions of Huawei continue, in the United Kingdom as in France, to provoke great perplexity: the British Parliament in 2013 denounced the "facility with which the government of London has opened the door to a group whose technology apparently poses a security problem to the United Kingdom." The authors of the House of Commons' Intelligence and Security Committee report added, "While we are reassured by GCHQ [Government Communications Headquarters]'s confidence in BT [British Telecom], we note that they acknowledge that the risk of unauthorized access cannot be entirely eliminated."[49]

TWO

SPREADING THE TENTACLES, OPPORTUNISTICALLY

Whether public or private, Chinese groups that invest in Europe often have the support of the Chinese state. Though no sector escapes their hunger for acquisitions on the continent, there are three main areas of focus: tourism, real estate, and technology. But the results in these different areas have been varied.

When China wakes up to traveling, Europe will be richer. Well after Napoleon's audacious prediction, "When China wakes up, the world will tremble," the reality of Chinese tourism has finally lent substance to the famous saying. Both purveyors, such as the French department store Galleries Lafayette, ubiquitous in airport duty-free shopping malls, available through concierge services in hotels, and even to be accessed courtesy of the French administration, which since January 2014 has provided short-stay visas within forty-eight hours of applying, and those employed in the European hospitality business are experiencing unprecedented change: they must look Chinese as quickly as they can or risk not profiting from this particular

"Great Leap Forward." The European capitals are already the principal destinations of millions of Chinese visitors.[1] To many Chinese
tourists, Europe seems like an immense museum and Europeans
appear barely to work, seemingly spending most of their time on
vacation, in cafés, or in luxury boutiques. But now the luxury clients are the Chinese tourists themselves. Since 2013 they have been
the leading buyers of duty-free products. On average, each Chinese
tourist spends up to €1,000 on gifts each trip, or twice as much as
for lodging and meals.

The investment picture is changing now as well. Apart from the
great Asian hotels that have opened in Paris in recent years, several
Chinese groups have acquired hotels in Paris, such as the Hôtel du
Collectionneur, which was discreetly bought by the Export-Import
Bank of China (often called the China Exim Bank). Hainan province's HNA Group in 2014 bought the French airline Aigle Azur and
the Spanish hotel management company NH Group, which has
properties in Europe, Africa, and North America. Greece, a country little visited until now, in 2014 welcomed 40,000 Chinese tourists, drawn by the Chinese television series *Beijing Love Story* and
its romantic rendezvous in Greece. And Dalian Wanda, having earlier bought the British luxury yacht firm Sunseeker for £300 million,
will soon have a five-star hotel in London.

For China, which for some years now has been increasingly ex-
ploring the leisure lifestyle, tourism and resorts are a key sector for
business investment. It is not by chance that Fosun Group bought
Club Med in 2015, for the purpose of opening vacation villages
from the north to the south of China.

From the Warsaw-Berlin highway construction contract, granted
to the Chinese in 2009, then withdrawn in 2011 by the Polish government, to massive investments in the shipping ports and transpor-
tation hubs of Athens, to the purchase of shares in public services
(such as electricity in Portugal) and of London real estate, the leading edge of the wave of Chinese investment in Europe suggests a
conquest of the West by concrete, brick, cement, and asphalt.

There is a Chinese tradition that investment in real estate opens the way, and this has been a constant since the start of capitalism. This model seems to apply at the international level: a study by the Savills brokerage house found that in 2013, fewer than 10 percent of wealthy Westerners spent their fortune on real estate, whereas 30 percent of wealthy Chinese did so.[2] Another study published around the same time reported that Chinese buyers influenced the market for new real estate more than any other group did.[3] A draw for such investors is that several European countries offer long-stay residence cards—good for five or ten years, depending on the actual investment amount and the particular country's policy—to those who acquire real estate. Several thousand individuals have already benefited from these offers.

But it is important to observe closely the major state and private actors to get a complete view of the situation. Once Chinese business entities achieve a critical size in their domestic market, they tend to take an interest in international real estate. Thus, many state companies have acquired European headquarters: Paris was chosen by the China Exim Bank and the Commercial Aircraft Corporation of China (COMAC), for example. Two of the three largest public institutional investment funds, the China Investment Corporation and the State Authority for Foreign Exchange (SAFE), have been authorized to place their assets in secure investments.

The growing number of newly minted millionaires has been joined by actors with even more consequential means. The latter include major Chinese real estate groups, which, after achieving a dominant position in their own market, move out of their usual territory to diversify their portfolios, and state-owned enterprises (SOEs), which always want to own at least the buildings in which they are housed (see figure 2-1).

Experts in these economic sectors estimate that China manages tens of billions of euros in real estate, mostly in Asia. As a sign of the attraction in 2012 and the flood of investors into Europe, the special administrative region of Hong Kong established an unprecedented

FIGURE 2-1. *Chinese Foreign Direct Investment by Type of Investor, 2000–14*

SOURCE: *Rhodium Group/Baker & McKenzie, "Reaching New Heights: An Update on Chinese Investments in Europe," 2015.*

tax on any transaction emanating from a nonresident, a step unheard of in this paradise of free trade. Investment in other Asian Pacific cities, such as Bangkok, Kuala Lumpur, and Sydney, follows more slowly, but on the same trajectory: sooner or later China will become an actor that cannot be ignored.

In the West, the second wave of investment is well under way: in less than three years at least €10 billion have been invested in the purchase of land, buildings, and commercial centers. Famous buildings have gone to Chinese investment groups, among them the iconic General Motors Building in Manhattan, which was sold in 2013 to a consortium comprising Boston Properties, the family of Zhang Xin, chief executive of Soho China, and Brazil's Safra banking company, as well as new construction, such as the two residential towers in San Francisco. SAFE has acquired four office blocks in the City of London.

Unlike their competitors from Qatar or Singapore, Chinese investors are active, fluid, and potentially numerous. They buy, sell, and exchange large volumes of goods over a short time period and are capable of destabilizing a market with a few operations. In addition to buying up venerable properties and sometimes building new ones, some Chinese groups seek to develop whole neighborhoods for commercial, financial, or even cultural purposes. One project, exceeding €1 billion, that was launched in mid-2013 in London entailed the complete renovation of fourteen hectares around London's city airport to create a third financial center in the capital. The advance figures referred to 20,000 jobs to be filled and an investment of €9 billion in the British economy. A new kind of Chinatown may be emerging.[4]

Outside London, the Chinese have been prudent in the rest of Europe. In Paris, a major Parisian agency offered Chinese investors a building from the Haussmann era for €100 million, without success. It was too ostentatious, the investors said, preferring more discreet purchases. In this connection, the purchase in 2013 of a mansion (*hôtel particulier*) for €12 million by the largest Chinese producer of alcohol, the Maotai Group, and the purchase of the Marriott Hotel on the Champs-Élysées for €344.5 million in June 2014 by a cousin of the former Chinese president Hu Jintao, both solid, unremarkable purchases, should be noted. A Paris project that did not go through was SAFE's attempted acquisition of the Beaugrenelle commercial center in Paris's 15th arrondissement, along the Seine, for an estimated €700 million.[5] The usual pitfalls—language difficulties, complex legal and social administration, heavy taxes, and mediocre returns on investment—likely restrained the Chinese investors' hand. Nor are they jet-setters, looking for purchases along the Mediterranean or in the mountains, preferring luxury hotels in the tropics.

The experience and subsequent enlightenment of Myra Chan illustrates this situation. A banker in Hong Kong who transferred to Paris in 2010 as a key figure in the China branch of the luxury real estate agency Barnes, she set up an entire arsenal of activities and forums to attract a Chinese clientele: seminars in France and in China, presentations in salons, brochures, blogs, television programs, even the support of some celebrities, all to no avail. There were hours of secret meetings and visits to properties of all kinds, but not a single transaction was finalized. Chan then turned to event planning, organizing upscale leisure and discovery trips for Chinese businessmen, fleeting and glittery, and that went better.

INFRASTRUCTURE

Investing in real property—the "stone touch"—has been the almost exclusive privilege of London. Elsewhere in Europe the Chinese positioning in infrastructure is concentrated on the periphery, in Greece, Portugal, and Eastern Europe (figure 2-2). For the latter, the recipe is neither new nor surprising on the part of a formerly communist country that knows how to construct and manage large projects at extremely competitive costs and is strong in abundant, cheap labor, which can be exploited at will, not to mention advantageous financing. This ensemble, tested many times on the Chinese market, was first successfully exported to neighboring countries, then to Africa, before being extended from Ukraine to Poland via Serbia, Romania, and Hungary.

Railroad lines, highways, electricity generation, bridges: the possibilities are numerous for a set of Chinese technologies and the kinds of expertise that are sufficiently advanced and able to satisfy countries that want to catch up with their neighbors in Western Europe. For the Chinese, these transactions are truly "win-win," as the prized formula has it.[6]

More controversial and worrying is the rise of Chinese presence in Belarus and Ukraine through China's participation in two gigantic projects that now face an uncertain future, owing to political tensions in the region. On two occasions in 2013 separated by an interval of several months, China promised to invest more than €10 billion to build a new industrial town on 1,000 square kilometers of waste ground near Minsk, and to buy no less than 30,000 square kilometers of arable land (equivalent to Belgium in size) on a fifty-year lease, a mere 100,000 hectares (1,000 square kilometers) of

FIGURE 2-2. *Top Fifteen Sectors Invested in EU Countries, 2000–14*

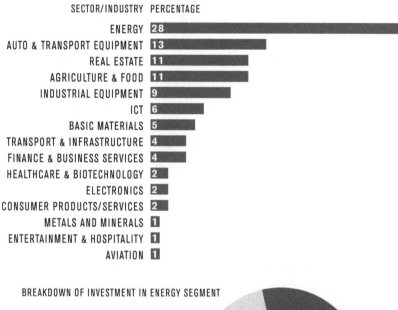

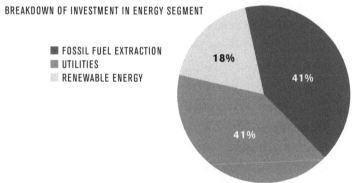

BREAKDOWN OF INVESTMENT IN ENERGY SEGMENT

SOURCE: *Rhodium Group/Baker & McKenzie, "Reaching New Heights: An Update on Chinese Investments in Europe,"* 2015.

which were to take the form of a pig farm. Rarely have such sums and ambitions been united to achieve such economic control and such foreign political and strategic interference in a third country. It remains to be seen whether the region's geopolitics will permit the realization of this project.

In Western Europe, it appears inconceivable that Chinese groups would be interested in major civil engineering projects as constructors of major public works, or that they have managed to become owners of agricultural land. The announcement that a Chinese consortium led by a subsidiary of the China Railway Group was interested in the renovation of a section of the line HS2—a link between Birmingham and its airport as a portion of the complete high-speed line between London and Manchester—surprised many experts. A memorandum of understanding was signed between China and the United Kingdom. Similarly, in the United States, the China Railway Stock Corporation announced in the summer of 2015 a $60 million investment in a plant in Springfield, Massachusetts, that will assemble new cars for Boston's subway system.[7]

Midway between the "classic" Chinese advances in the former satellites of the old Soviet empire and those less ordinary ones in two countries still under Russian influence, we find minority shares in port and electric infrastructure, including in nuclear power generation. These investments demonstrate the internationalization of jobs and the important role played by Chinese actors. Apart from investment in Athens's Port of Piraeus (€500 million) and participation in the utility company Energias de Portugal (€2.7 billion), both mentioned in chapter 1, a consortium of two of the three national state-owned leaders—the China General Nuclear Power Group (CGNPG), in association with its rival, China National Nuclear Corporation (CNNC)—got together £6 billion to construct one or more nuclear power stations of the emergency reaction protector type in collaboration with the EDF in the United Kingdom. Some formal but undetailed agreements were also signed in late 2015 between those two SOEs and EDF-Areva to possibly take significant stakes in two of Areva's key businesses.

These major projects have given rise to a model that is bound to be repeated, under two types of scenario. The first type is a forced opening. The global recession of 2008–09 obliged the Greek government to sell shares as fast as possible and therefore cheaply, just as the colossal debt and the lack of funds in state companies forced the Portuguese authorities to open that country's capital to foreign investors. The newly managed full competition between public services and the extra expenditures that must be borne by any new nuclear generating station after the Fukushima disaster have also prompted Western entities to consider other types of partnerships; the classic process of a call for partners and a search for allies of circumstance is quickly revived. The second scenario is the deployment of the red carpet. For any initiate, winning a call for tender is a true challenge, since the alchemy between the material proposition and the political and relational aspects appears complex. The Chinese are becoming excellent players of this game. They often win the hand by playing up the purchase price and dangling before their counterparties the inducement of access to the Chinese market, usually so difficult to open. China thus swoops up the deal.

The gamble of investments desired by the Chinese is often linked to possible transfers of technology. And when the infrastructure is not of prime national importance, the Chinese presence often proves salutary. In Athens, the state-owned China Ocean Shipping Company (COSCO) has not only acquired dedicated container terminals, it has irreversibly transformed the operating mode of port infrastructure in all of Greece. Henceforth Chinese-style management will focus on tighter cost control and long-term development. The victory of the Greek left with Syriza's election victory in January 2015 was a boon for the unions, which oppose any restriction of the right to work, but in this respect the unions and union-free Chinese management style are on a collision path.

On the other hand, when the stakes are nationally sensitive, tensions can rise quickly. In the great majority of European countries the sale of national infrastructure to Chinese investors is viewed poorly. This is especially true in France, where the purchase of 49.9 percent of the Toulouse-Blagnac Airport at the end of 2014 was met with a general outcry. Karine Berger, a legislator responsible for economic issues in the Socialist Party, declared she was "not at all easy" about the sale of this airport to a non-European investor.[8] But the visit of Prime Minister Manuel Valls to China, followed by Li Keqiang's visits to Paris and Toulouse, seemed to calm things down. "How could we sell the Airbus to China and prevent investment from China?" queried Valls in an interview.[9] The European public needs to be convinced, and is far from being converted.[10]

INDUSTRIES AND TECHNOLOGIES: SERVING THE CHINESE MARKET

For the Chinese, one overriding question remains in the industrial sector: how to obtain more technology transfers from Europeans. From steam shovels to industrial pumps, from silicone resins to polyurethane fibers, and on through cereal bars, milk powder, and household appliances: it is not easy at first glance to follow the red thread of Chinese industrial implantation in Europe, apart from the examples already cited in this book. What might be the common theme of Chinese investments in the chemical, food-processing, civil engineering, and consumer goods industries? And how might a partial sinicization of these sectors change the situation in Europe as well as in China?

To understand the need for technology, we have to go back to China. In a number of realms, the domestic market has for the past fifteen years been advancing at a frenetic pace, prompting the major Chinese business groups to pursue development at the national level. On the Chinese market, the local context offers "facilities" (relational, proximity, price), but the competition is lively. Therefore the technological aspects assume great importance.

Many Chinese enterprises eventually find it necessary to cross borders to identify target markets with technological assets. Continental Europe, led by France and Germany, is recognized for its innovative and high-performance products, and many European enterprises have become well established in China, which often facilitates the task of researching locations. Chinese delegations then go on the offensive and search the continent, meeting various actors in the technology sector and sometimes setting up partnerships oriented toward the sharing of recent-generation patents and procedures. This approach is executed not through consultancy firms, business banks, or lawyers but rather through a social network of friends and acquaintances, and through governmental or political missions in the towns, cities, or provinces where the enterprises are situated.

From the perspective of the coveted targets, the openness of Chinese investors is limited. The business mandate not to neglect such unique opportunities invites corporations to look more closely, and many of them actively countenance a deal. Enterprises that do tend to be those dependent on the European market, which offers limited growth possibilities and few significant economies of scale. Thus China appears to offer an opportunity for growth, but it is difficult to gain access unless a Chinese partner can be found. Corporations may also face strong pressure from their important shareholders, whether families, highly rated groups, or investment funds, that welcome a Chinese alliance and want to sell at the best moment, before it's too late.

The experiences of Sany, Zoomlion, and the Xuzhou Construction Group are representative of this game of Go between hunters and prey. These three enterprises are among the five major Chinese corporations that have made their way to the top in the machine tool market (civil engineering). Faced with strong local competition and the success of Western industry leaders like Caterpillar, they understand that their health depends on developing a partnership outside China. Xuzhou Construction was the fastest off the mark but the unluckiest: back in 2005 it hoped to attract the American Carlyle Group into its capital at 85 percent and thereby profit from its relationships and expertise. The proposed move was too early for the Chinese administration, which could not accept the involvement of such a renowned entity that would transform, radically and irreversibly, the companies it took over; moreover, the Carlyle Group was already listed on the stock exchange (because such listing strengthens the public side of the deal, it becomes less attractive to Chinese investors). The bargaining and talks went on for three years, but nothing eventuated. Finally, Xuzhou Construction concluded a joint venture with a Korean competitor, Doosan, which bought up the bulk of the capital of Schwing, a large German manufacturer of concrete pumps, in 2012.

By contrast, the trajectory of the negotiations by ChemChina-BlueStar in the course of three huge successive acquisitions between 2006 and 2011—those of Adisseo, Rhodia Silicons, and Elkem, for a total of more than €3 billion—is an example of success. The first two operations were laborious, inasmuch as relations between the French teams and their Chinese partners were strained (the Chinese engineers barely spoke English and knew little of markets and practices outside China), and the negotiators were given a rough ride by diktats from the Chinese bosses, often delivered at a distance. The third investment, though, was executed without any real operational or intercultural obstacles, thanks to intelligently used intermediaries.

An identical scenario played out for the Shanghai food-processing giant Bright Food, which admitted publicly to at least four failed transactions before it finally successfully nailed two. After the resounding failure of its attempts to buy CSR Sugar, Yoplait, GNC, and United Biscuits, in 2012 and 2013 it acquired, without much difficulty, the Australian firm Manassen for the sum of €400 million, before also pocketing the British group Weetabix and its famous cereals for £1.2 billion. In addition, Bright Food has taken a controlling interest in the famous Italian olive oil company Salov. According to internal sources, the transaction with the owner, the global investment fund Lion Capital, was done Western style and included integrating the "goodwill" specific to the brand into its valuation.

After the potential traps of mergers and acquisitions have been negotiated successfully, the most complex part of the process still

remains to be done: integrating two parties in such a way as to realize gains and synergies as fast as possible. Globally, more than one
transaction in two underperforms the expectations of investors, and
may even lose value. What is the situation today for these Chinese
enterprises and their new European beachheads?

The assessment is mixed, and could be summarized with three
categories: (1) the game of technology transfer from Europe to
China is only partially successful, and more complex than anticipated; (2) strategic or operational changes in the firms acquired by
their new owners are astonishingly few, or at least not obvious; and
(3) domination by the more powerful and better-armed groups beyond their common borders is still awaited.

Technologically speaking, the rapprochement of Zoomlion and
Compagnia Italiana Forme Acciaio (CIFA) raises a scenario about
the initial letter of intent. After five years of life together the two
enterprises, now combined, were better than ever and had accomplished the true miracle of successful integration: knowing how to
profit from one another. Zoomlion was able to benefit from the
technological advances of the Italian company to go upscale with a
broad array of construction equipment. A recent study by the brokerage company CLSA, a specialist in Asian markets, confirms the
fact: a two-week professional test of ten Chinese excavators and
the best manufacturers in the world (Caterpillar, Komatsu, Hita-
chi, Doosan, and Komalco) with respect to three major attributes,
reliability, productivity, and energy efficiency, rated the Chinese
machinery just below Caterpillar's but above the Korean and Japanese competition. CIFA is durably established in China in niche
segments, thanks to the distribution network and the commercial
efforts of its parent company.

The silicon division of ChemChina-BlueStar represents the other
face of the coin. Much less adept than Zoomlion/CIFA, it tried hard
to capitalize on the most advanced technologies of its Lyon subsidiary.
The reasons for its indifferent success are many: installation of the
most recent-generation procedures in advanced chemical processes

is complex, costly, and requires state-of-the art human expertise and technology. The highly qualified European engineers recruited for this purpose, who had to expatriate themselves for long periods at a time, tended to have poor relationships with local personnel, who often were barely receptive. Then too, the market hardened, reducing margins and fostering a status quo more profitable in the short term.

Though technological competence has sometime crossed borders, organizational transfers are less frequent. When new Chinese owners are installed, many European managers in place find they have poorly anticipated the situation with their Chinese shareholders, who are typically effaced, if not made invisible, and the European managers often have to leave. In certain industrial sectors (apart from the sales arms of Haier, ZTE, or Huawei, for example), few Chinese managers are sent to Europe. Instead, younger recruits are preferred who are at ease in English and comfortable with prolonged training. At first, European managers and department heads remain in place and are responsible for conveying important messages by interacting with the head office, including going there regularly. Chinese staff members often replace them eventually, but on the whole the staffing seems incomplete. By the same token, few European managers transfer from a European subsidiary to the mother ship in China.

These intercultural difficulties make a Chinese conquest of the West a bold, even risky, proposition. How do you conquer the planet if you do not want to assemble the talent? How can you be a global actor?

The view of Asleigh Ogier, former director of international development at the tunnel builder NFM Technologies, a small company in the Lyon area, owned by Shenyang Heavy Industries Corporation since 2009, projects patience and circumspection: "Since the merger, we have indeed won some worksites outside Europe and China by combining French savoir faire and Chinese labor. But in China our expertise is not yet recognized, whereas here any tunnel project has to be done without foregrounding the links with China, for fear of losing the contract. The synergies are unfortunately limited and we really have the impression of not advancing like a single group but rather like two entities each living its own life. We can never become a world leader that way."[11]

THE AUTOMOBILE INDUSTRY: A UNIQUE CASE?

Never has an industry as important as cars so interested China, yet the sector is still far from being dominated by Chinese companies. Faced with the need to realize the success factors common to all businesses, including finding the maximum critical size, auto manufacturers are forming alliances to gain an optimal share of the common platforms while racing each other for growth. The battle is being fought in three dimensions: in the Chinese market, between Chinese companies, and for the low-cost car, to which is added a hint of the car of the future, whether hybrid, electric, or touch command.

Two stakes specific to China's gaining a foothold in the European auto market are (1) the imbalance between supply and demand, which is much more pronounced in Europe than in the United States, and (2) the notorious differences between one country and another within Europe, which add additional levels of complexity. For the past decade, foreign car manufacturers have known that they are playing for their survival in China. China's domestic demand, with more than 20 million vehicles purchased in 2013, makes China the largest market in the world, with growth rates in the double digits. All the industry leaders are established in China and generate a business there that is both large and profitable. However, they are all joint ventures (at 50-50) with the six huge SOEs—FAW (Jilin), SAIC (Shanghai), Dongfeng (Wuhan), BIAC (Beijing), GAC (Guangzhou), and Chang An (Nanjing)—and divide up the large pie accordingly; there are as well three smaller companies that are considered private, Geely, Chery, and Great Wall Motors. Their success is not identical: BMW and Mercedes-Benz are well anchored at the premium end, while General Motors, Volkswagen, and Toyota dominate the sector, followed by Honda, Kia-Hyundai and PSA, Ford, Renault-Nissan, and Fiat-Chrysler. A single European player, the Volkswagen Group, feasts at the head of the table and holds the lead, without blinking an eye at its Chinese partners.

Though these Chinese automobile groups, whether state-owned or private, yesterday were lagging behind or nonexistent, they now have the singular ambition of taking advantage of their respective assets, their colossal war booty, and their capacity to occupy segments of the market that are growing strongly (principally SUVs and low-cost cars) to ramp up their international presence aggressively. They are also undoubtedly seeking means of growth, recognition, and advanced technologies.

Apart from the stranglehold, which is somewhat anecdotal, of Geely over the holding company handling London taxis in 2007 and the many attempts by various Chinese entities to buy all or part of Saab, it was the Shanghai group SAIC that successfully launched the first worldwide operation. SAIC benefited from the difficulties of the American giant General Motors in 2009 and assumed participation in GM's recapitalization plan during its introduction to Wall Street the following year. The agreement to share the most advanced American technology with China called for a joint company to design small cars based in China. The arrangement aimed at markets in emerging countries, at the entry of SAIC into the Indian subsidiary of GM at 50 percent, and at the opening of the British network of GM to the Chinese partner. It is commonly thought that this GM-SAIC alliance has obliged GM to withdraw its participation in the capital of the French PSA Peugeot-Citroën.

In Europe, the sale of the iconic Swedish brand Volvo (which was then in collapse) by Ford to the Chinese Geely for close to €2 billion in 2010 made a big splash. What could be expected from a marriage between a hot-blooded firm under the direction of Li

Shufu, its fiery boss, and his Swedish counterpart, reputedly cold and distant?

Four years later, the hour of the first review came around. In 2010, three principal strategic goals were enunciated to justify the $11 billion invested in the short term: (1) to float Volvo and to ensure priority deployment in China and in the United States; (2) in the medium term (by 2014) to produce cars in China by benefiting from a more competitive cost basis (a 25 to 30 percent saving realized on the principal components) and to launch several new high-end models dedicated to this market; and (3) in the longer term (by 2017) to create common mid-range models allying Swedish savoir faire with Chinese competitiveness, whose market would be world-wide. In the end, the Geely Group succeeded in integrating an iconic brand and being very profitable.

The first objective was partially reached with the production of 450,000 vehicles in 2013. After catastrophic losses in 2010 and 2011 and severe ones in 2012, a barely positive bottom line was achieved in 2013. Europe still represented almost 80 percent of Geely's market, and China and the United States split the remaining 20 percent in equal proportion—far from the envisioned 60-20-20 division of the market. The second objective awaited fruition after the launch of the new model SUV XC90, entirely conceived in Sweden but produced in China on brand-new assembly lines.[12]

The third objective is still being worked on and is the subject of much bargaining. Negotiating the ideal compromise between building medium-range cars faithful to the Volvo tradition and accommodating the needs of the Chinese market is a perilous exercise. Discussions at the highest level seem to have softened, though they are characterized by an almost permanent tug-of-war between a European management that is attached to its traditional roots and a Chinese CEO who insists on a radical and ongoing orientation toward a sinicization of models.

The third major Chinese transaction in the European automotive industry occurred in 2013, when Dongfeng took a 14 percent participation, alongside the French state, in the capital of PSA Peugeot-Citroën, for €800 million.

Did this transaction represent the ineluctable taking of control by a Chinese SOE of one of the most illustrious French family firms, or was it simply a marriage of convenience between two heavy-weights of the automobile industry with a common goal? Perhaps a bit of both.[13] Even if the purchase price was a very good financial operation for Dongfeng, PSA's partnership in China was the company's sole savior for more than fifteen years. Dongfeng will probably become in time the main shareholder, as the French state does not have the inclination or the means to remain so. And it is unlikely that the Peugeot family has the funds to compete with Dongfeng in the next wave of financing and recapitalization. In the short term, the two entities have every interest in getting along well together, given their respective ambitions and limits: a battered PSA is obliged to remake its health in Europe while accelerating the development of other markets; Dongfeng is absent at the international level and needs that exposure. What the Chinese bring (Dongfeng, plus credits from Chinese banks) should facilitate a restructuring that gives priority to a common investment aimed at producing low-cost cars in Southeast Asia.

Beyond these capitalist considerations, what can be said about the gradual arrival of Chinese automobiles in Europe? Until recently, the launches were slow in coming, but that could change rapidly.[14] However, three facts invite caution. First, Kia, the low-cost subsidiary of the Korean firm Hyundai, is among the entities counting on the European market, and nobody would have bet on it five years ago. Second, and counterposed to the first fact, Geely (like Chery) is unrelentingly pursuing its investments in Eastern Europe and since January 2014 has held the largest share of the market in Belarus and Ukraine. And third, the most threatening actor may be Qoros—the original partnership between Chery and Israel Corporation—an enterprise run by former professionals from Volkswagen, BMW, and other venerable firms. The Qoros 3 model is the only compact

Chinese car ever to have received a five-star rating from Euro NCAP on professional safety testing. A first concession opened in Slovakia in 2015, where Qoros was betting on first-year sales of 15,000 vehicles.

THE ART OF LIVING: A FLASH IN THE PAN?

By 2014, China and its consumers were decisively at the top of the luxury market, in areas ranging from alcoholic drinks to clothing to works of art. The spring semi-annual study by Bain Consulting dedicated exclusively to luxury goods confirmed that the Chinese held 29 percent of this market,[15] while the *Economist* explained in some depth that the Chinese consumer was the prime mover of most mass consumption products.[16] The prestigious British auction houses Sotheby's and Christie's have also noted that Hong Kong and China have become together the world's third auction market, after the United States and the United Kingdom. There is nothing to prevent a legacy auction firm from one day flying the Chinese colors. It is widely recognized that a few Chinese companies (notably Poly Auction, a subsidiary of the People's Liberation Army), until recently unknown, now dominate the rather isolated Chinese market in luxury and are assuming importance in Hong Kong.

At the European level, will the ferment around companies whose products are devoted to the art of living translate into a myriad of Chinese investments? Week after week the press reports on Chinese investments in French vineyards, for example. But how much weight do these investments actually carry?

The internationalization of vineyards in Bordeaux, once an English duchy, is far from a recent phenomenon, since exporting was developed in the thirteenth century, largely to England. Though the Chinese began to invest little by little in 2008, acquiring properties of less than €5 million at the start, the trend rapidly built to a fever pitch, with recent transactions involving around €30 million. Forty-some

Bordeaux properties are today owned by Chinese businessmen or financial groups. And Bordeaux producers constantly enthuse about their success in the Middle Kingdom, which now imports 10 percent of the wine produced in the Gironde; by contrast, the Chinese consumed almost no wine in 2000.[17]

Because France has more than 8,000 wine châteaux, however, these figures argue for prudence in interpreting the Chinese presence in the vineyards. It would be unreasonable to speak of a Chinese conquest, even a very slight one, of the French wine establishment, especially since, exclusive of the three acquisitions realized by the alcohol giants COFCO and Maotai, all purchases have been made by wealthy individuals in search of exotic and quick adventure. A cautionary tale concerns the drama surrounding the sale of the Château de La Rivière, near Libourne, at the end of 2013. When the transaction was complete, the Chinese buyer, the Hong Kong billionaire Lam Kok (head of Brilliant Group, a company specializing in tea), and the French vendor, James Grégoire, along with the new owner's son and an interpreter, took a helicopter flight over the property that ended in a fatal crash. The news went viral on the Chinese social media, and Mr. Kok's dream of creating a focus for cultural exchanges around tea and wine did not see the light of day.

More relevant is the translation of these vineyard purchases to Chinese territory, which very much resembles the commercial actions and investments of French investors in China (such as Pernod Ricard in the 1990s). What is happening is less a sinicization of Bordeaux vineyards than a partial frenchification of the Chinese wine market. Not only do local (French) teams remain in control, they also travel more and more frequently to China to educate and cultivate the public's taste for fine bottles. Wine boutiques are opening in major Chinese cities, often managed by entrepreneurs who have been educated in France. In Shanghai, one no longer counts the number of wine schools or specialist magazines or dedicated Internet sites. Almost 160 châteaux have been set up across China, and 200 more are under construction. Some of them are owned jointly with European investors such as the French group Castel.

By contrast, in the world of ready-made clothing, accessories, watches, and jewelry, Chinese interest in European manufacturers must be assessed as meager to nonexistent; the only activity of note has been the repeated purchases by the Hong Kong group Li & Fung (through its subsidiary, Trinity) of small European companies in difficulty (such as Geeve & Hawkes, Cerruti 1881, Sonia Rykiel, Robert Clergerie, and Delvaux). Only a few Chinese enterprises have become caught up in the acquisition game, mainly Fosun, which took a 10 percent share of the Greek jewelry company Folli Follie for €85 million in 2011 and a 35 percent share of the famous Italian fashion house Raffaelle Caruso in 2013.

INDUSTRIAL PARKS IN EUROPE: AN UNFULFILLED CHINESE AMBITION

No discussion of the spectacular growth of Chinese business would be complete without a mention of industrial parks. Since the first four special economic zones were created at the end of the 1970s in southern China (in Shenzhen, Xiamen, Zhuhai, and Shantou), they have mushroomed in the four corners of China and welcome a large number of multinational corporations. The recipe is simple and unchanging. Each city constructs one to several enclosed malls that are managed professionally and offer a quality infrastructure and significant tax advantages, as well as aid in the form of a complex array of administrative and logistical services. The goal is to attract foreign investors who will feel comfortable in the mall and consequently be disposed to pay rent and charges. In addition to factories and office buildings, schools, hospitals, and hotels spring up in most of them, as do a good number of local clients and suppliers. These "platforms," created from nothing, effectively form a city within the city and may prove profitable in a few years. Some of them are even quoted on the stock exchange.

On the basis of this success, several Chinese businessmen have seized on the formula and tried to export it to Europe, wagering that Chinese firms will also prove interested and will bring along their clients, suppliers, and Western partners, just as they have done in the Chinese megamalls. Potential partners in Europe include local and regional authorities, which are always on the lookout for new ideas in a time of scarcity.

In 2015, more than fifty such industrial parks were on the record books in Europe, in sites ranging from Finland to Italy and from Ireland to Poland, but they were not doing well. According to an analysis conducted by the University of Leeds, most of them were underutilized or had not got off the ground. The study's author, Professor Hinrich Voss, said in an interview that "these hubs are above all the fruit of real estate promoters without a real industrial project who often profit from generous conditions for implantation in remote zones. The Chinese clientele is not yet sufficient and is being solicited by too many sites."[18]

The examples of sites in the Moselle and in Indre largely substantiate this view. Construction on the Comex project in Thionville, in eastern France, baptized as ITEC and first announced in 2012, was halted, then partially restarted.[19] Construction of the mall in Châteauroux proceeds slowly, with the first serious advance coming in June 2014, after five years of procrastination, when local officials and Chinese representatives laid the cornerstone of an office building for a new Franco-Chinese business zone in Ozans. A building of 4,400 square meters will be placed in service. Called Eurosity, it is intended to be the "first Sino-European hub for economic cooperation." Two Chinese firms, Huawei and Sanei, and the French firm Aformac are the first tenants. Huawei, never backfooted in making announcements (which are not always followed by results, a point underscored by the affair of the research center in 2009 with its 200 fictional jobs), says it wants to establish a training center in Eurosity for its clients. The elevator manufacturer Sanei plans to set up a demonstration hall and a center for customer relations for its clients throughout Europe. Further real developments are awaited in Eurosity and in the other industrial parks, whose fortunes seem to be languishing.

THREE

A NEW KIND OF MULTINATIONAL CORPORATION

The photograph on the front page of *China Daily*, the official Chinese newspaper in English, published and distributed in six world capitals, said more than the article accompanying it. Two well-known figures are shown conversing at the World Economic Forum in Davos, where the political and economic elites gather each year in January. Wang Jianlin, chairman of the Dalian Wanda Group and the richest person in China, is speaking, while on his right, British prime minister David Cameron leans toward him, listening intently, apparently fascinated.[1]

An unknown figure in the West before 2012, when he became owner of the giant American cinema chain AMC for almost €2 billion, Wang Jianlin announced his desire to participate in more than €3 billion of financing of cogeneration plants, after investing heavily in the United Kingdom, paying €1 billion for a sixty-two-story hotel and residential-use tower and €500 million to buy the British luxury yacht maker Sunseeker, which was in difficulty.[2] Wanda was also the chief real estate promoter investing in Spain in June 2014 through the purchase of the Edificio España for the tidy sum of €265 million. "Internationalization is a state of mind, you have to be prepared," Wang said in an interview.[3] Wang does not speak English and has never lived abroad.

The emergence of Chinese multinationals of a new kind, ready to conquer Europe, seems evident, as attested by the forward-facing stances of three large entities. The first example is the telecommunications infrastructure group Huawei, which has an annual turnover of almost €5 billion and a staff of 7,500 in Europe. In April 2014, Huawei's founder, Ren Zhengfei, compared the challenges of running his enterprise with those of the automaker BMW. The second testimonial is the open ambition of the leading appliances company Haier to double its share of the European market, from 4 percent to 8 percent, in five years, with only two factories, in Italy and Poland. And the third is the media's unveiling in London in February 2014 of the China Bright Food's stream of future investments in Europe.

The pronouncements of these Chinese companies and their chances of success may be understood in many ways. A dual-perspective review helps answer two important questions: What is the red thread sustaining the international (external) development of these Chinese groups? And how does their growth trajectory resemble that of their Western, Korean, or Japanese equivalents or show similarities to the major family groups of the Chinese diaspora?

Many studies have explored how enterprises originating in the new world powers advance and grow. This chapter analyzes the different models of success, concentrating on five principal ones that help expose the trajectories of Chinese companies that have set up shop in Europe. The five models are summarized in table 3-1, along with examples of each.

Haier illustrates the first type of strategy, that of moving from cheap products to more sophisticated ones. In the beginning, this group, based in Qingdao, concentrated on products that were copies of existing products (Western, if not Japanese and Korean) and that could be fabricated more cheaply in China and sold in under-

TABLE 3-1. *Chinese Multinational Corporations'*
Overseas Development Models

STRATEGY AND INTERNATIONALIZATION OPERATING MODEL	EXAMPLE	CHINESE SPECIFICITY
1. From cheap products to sophisticated ones	Haier	Weak
2. From OEM to client-direct approach[a]	Huawei	Medium
3. Massive acquisitions campaign	Lenovo, Fosun, Geely, ChemChina, Bright Dairy	High
4. "Orientalism"	Mandarin Oriental, Peninsula Hotel, Shangri-La Hotel (luxury hospitality)	Very high
5. National leaders pushed into overseas markets	Dongfeng, SAIC	Very high

a. *OEM denotes original equipment manufacturer.*

served markets. It then gradually began making de novo innovative, high-quality products (in both manufacturing and services) that could be sold competitively not just in China but all over the world. This model is the most common of the five. It was followed by many Japanese and Korean multinational corporations in the 1960s to the 1990s.

The strategy of Huawei reflects the second type of thinking and operational mode. Starting from products made at competitive costs, Huawei moved from subcontracting, which offered low margins, to the much more profitable commercialization of its own products among companies in the telecommunications sector (British Telecom, Orange, Deutsche Telekom). More recently, products that are innovative and less costly have distinguished Huawei from its competitors. Other Chinese companies have followed this trajectory.

The third growth model involves increasing purchases of Western firms linked to the development of the Chinese enterprises, which was the signature move leading to the successful internationalization of Lenovo (computers), Geely (automobiles), Bright Dairy (foods), and ChemChina (industrial chemistry and tires).[4] This model is not specific to China, but the broader scope and greater scale of its realization in China are characteristic of China's corporate culture.

The fourth growth model is chiefly characterized by some of the five-star hotel groups based in Hong Kong. The model pursues a strategy nicely dubbed "Orientalist": the establishment of service companies that combine the professionalism of Western firm managers with ancestral Oriental savoir faire, all supported by cheaper labor costs. The arrival in Paris of three palatial hotels, the Shangri-La, the Mandarin, and the Peninsula, will undoubtedly force French hoteliers to adapt to this new landscape. Other companies that have implemented this strategy are the small, emerging companies that produce Chinese luxury brands, especially Shanghai Tang (taken over by the Swiss financial group Richemont), Icicle, Shang Xia (a brand launched by Hermès), and IT.

The fifth and last growth model is the almost exclusive privilege of Chinese state-owned enterprises (SOEs), including some in the automobile sector. Companies operationalizing this model venture beyond their borders by relying principally on dominating the domestic market and enjoying significant inputs of capital.

Whatever the principal growth model in place, Chinese groups always mix genres, sometimes following Western-style trajectories, sometimes modeling themselves on their Japanese or Korean equivalents or on the conglomerates in Hong Kong or Singapore—and then modifying the model in original ways. To illustrate and compare the different emphases of Western, Chinese, and Asia ex-Chinese companies, table 3-2 lists fifteen attributes characteristic of the development of major enterprises beyond their domestic borders. These fifteen attributes, which for China are conditioned by

TABLE 3-2. *Chinese Multinational Corporations Compared to Their Western and Asian Counterparts*

ATTRIBUTE	WESTERN MULTINATIONAL CORPORATIONS	TOYOTA AND SAMSUNG (JAPAN/KOREA)	CHEUNG KONG GROUP (HONG KONG)	CHINESE MULTINATIONAL CORPORATIONS
1. Big-size stance	■■■	■■■		■■■
2. Domestic leadership as a kick-off overseas lever	■■	■■■		■■■
3. Balance of domestic market and overseas market	■■■	■■■	■	■
4. Balance of developed markets and emerging markets	■■■	■■■	■	■■
5. Original products	■■■	■■■	■■	■
6. Branding	■■■	■■■	■■	■
7. R&D and innovation stance	■■■	■■■	■	■■■
8. Western-style corporate governance	■■■	■■■	■■	■■■
9. International management	■■■	■■	■	■
10. Autonomy and fair play	■■■	■■■	■■	■
11. Prominent leader with strong ambition	■■	■■■	■■■	■■■
12. External levers	■	■	■■■	■■■
13. Low-frill products	■	■	■■	■■■
14. Nonorganic growth over organic growth	■	■	■■■	■■■
15. Diversification	■	■	■■■	■■

SOURCE: *Alain Sepulchre.*

NOTE: *Number of bullets (one to three) indicates degree of expression of attribute.*

the reality of the Chinese experience in Europe, reveal strengths and weaknesses, opportunities and dangers, as well as possible factors that may limit firms' current and future success (for example, Chinese multinational corporations are rated low on the dimensions of fair play and bringing original products to market).

THREE STRENGTHS

To understand the philosophy of any Chinese enterprise, it is first necessary to meet its extraordinary leader, often its founder, who diverges substantially from the polished and technocratic image of Western, especially U.S., CEOs.

These leaders of Chinese multinationals are considered pioneers. Most now aged forty-five to seventy years, they were born and grew up in poor and remote provinces. (Jack Ma, the founder of the e-commerce giant Alibaba and a former English teacher in Hangzhou, Zhejiang's provincial capital, might be the exception that proves the rule.) These entrepreneurs arrived at the top by fighting hard, after enduring early experiences shaped by forces of circumstance. Then they got a foothold in a particular market by buying up for next to nothing one or more public assets "sold to order" by hard-pressed municipalities in the early 1980s. A major share of luck, allied with an uncommon work ethic, the ability to scheme, and an opportunistic disposition, enabled them to succeed. For them, the sky is the limit, and nothing can stop them except possibly a smear campaign mounted by hostile forces. (And in truth, the China of Xi Jinping has practiced selective denigration shamelessly for more than three years.)

Mixing with these personages during their jaunts outside China is both disconcerting and bedazzling. Poorly educated in every sense of the term, they are rough and feisty, but faithful and protective. Continually wary, they demand secrecy at all times, but they compensate their associates generously, as they do their personal bodyguards. Without any preestablished strategy or battle plan, they are quick as lightning when it comes to buying or to investing considerable sums of money. Their operational decisions, while not always rational, usually prove astonishingly correct and precise.

The Fosun Group and its four musketeers, led by its self-made boss, Guo Guangchang, is a perfect example. Students together in Shanghai at the prestigious Fudan University in the 1990s, without a cent to their name, the four pooled their meager savings and invested in sectors that were gradually opening up to competition, creating space for the emergence of private entities that performed much better. Beginning with medical kits, then moving on to the production and distribution of medicines, they were able to diversify, thanks to early profits made in real estate and in the steel sector. Financially strengthened by this war chest, they have more recently turned to financial services, the luxury market, and the "gray" economy, providing services to senior citizens. Within a few months, and essentially starting from nowhere, Fosun Group became an important actor in the insurance sector, first forming a joint venture in China with the British firm Prudential, then buying, in spring 2014, one of the largest Portuguese insurers, Caixa Seguros, for the tidy sum of €1 billion. In 2015, Fosun acquired the Portuguese bank Novo Banco.[5]

And Fosun knows how to do things in style. On a summery evening in June 2013 in Paris, those jostling on the quai André-Citroën to board the riverboat *Club Med* included the brand's CEO, Henri Giscard d'Estaing; the former French prime minister, Jean-Pierre Raffarin; and the CEOs of JCDecaux, Jean-Charles Decaux, and Société Générale, Frédéric Oudéa, all anticipating the first appearance in France of the China Entrepreneurs Club, brought over by Guo Guangchang. In the absence of a concrete business arrangement with these Chinese entrepreneurs during lean times for Europe, it was good for the major enterprises and for certain politicians to be seen in their company. The appearance of most of the Chinese guests, on the other hand, seemed out of place. Mr Zhang, dressed as a sailor, was toasted by a jovial Mr Wang, who addressed him as "captain."

Retired ambassador Wu Jianmin, who had officiated a ceremony earlier in the day at the Fondation Charles de Gaulle (the ceremony was in memory of the founder of the Fifth Republic, who recognized the People's Republic of China in 1964 and so is admired by the Chinese), had opted for a woodsman's jacket in red and black wool. "It is very interesting to invest in an enterprise like Club Med because it is not just real estate, it is long term, it is for the family," admiringly explained Liu Yonghao, chairman of the New Hope Group.

"I believe in Europe over the long term. With Club Med, we are committed to the future," Guo Guangchang asserted in an interview in Shanghai a few weeks later.[6] In Greece, he counts as assets the jeweler Folli Follies and a real estate and commercial complex whose construction will cost some €5 billion. "The Europeans want products that are less expensive, and the Chinese want brand names and technologies," added Guo, who claims he is "opposed to stereotypes." Yet in 2010 it was Fosun that disappointed investors when negotiations had already begun for participation in the capital of Barnes, the prestigious real estate agency that wished to enlarge its world footprint through developing an Asian clientele, which an alliance with Fosun in China would facilitate. The organizers of the operation still remember the limousines, the contracts prepared, the visits to villas, but nothing came of all that effort and circumstance, since the chairman of Fosun had disappeared, off on other frenetic adventures.

Without the vision and the appetite of these Chinese private entrepreneurs, however, nothing very concrete or significant sees the light of day in Europe. By contrast, Chinese state-owned enterprises (SOEs) are very often dependent on political decisions made at a much higher level. Their financing, of course, is very political and strategic.

CUTTING ONE'S TEETH ON THE DOMESTIC MARKET

Before conquering Europe, the Chinese companies that today are getting comfortably established on the continent had to conquer the

Chinese market, which is renowned for its complexity, roughness, and unpredictability. No Chinese enterprise has ever launched outside the national borders without having grown up locally and become, through its own efforts, a budding local giant.

This success takes time and requires many transformations in products, in operations, and in personnel training. From the first skirmishes in a small town to a position of dominance in one or more provinces is a veritable feat of arms. In China, emancipating oneself from a native village and clambering to get control of a clientele thousands of miles away is a much more perilous road than that taken by, say, a French enterprise trying to get a foothold in a neighboring country.

The history of Haier's struggle is revealing. Out of a hundred Chinese producers of refrigerators at the start of the 1990s, when Haier (then Qingdao Haier) first began to expand internationally through its partnership with the German firm Liebherr, only ten were still in business a decade later. Over the course of twenty years, Haier experimented with a series of marketing tools, in each case starting from scratch. The products were constantly adapted and improved, thanks to the targeted retention of major clients, a dedicated, round-the-clock after-sales service, and an unfailing organization that enabled delivery to thousands of points of sale by an independent subsidiary wholly dedicated to logistics. Certainly the visit to Germany of Haier's CEO, Zhang Ruimin, early in his career also contributed significantly to Haier's radical and visionary evolution.

These enterprises are also leaders because they have managed to survive in a competitive environment in which the battle for market share is often waged to the detriment of the margins. Institutional assistance, sometimes very prominent, has been able to favor one firm over another, but never in an ongoing or significant way. Consequently, enterprises successful on a national scale are armed with an array of experiences and talents, a useful and necessary prelude to expanding on the international scale.

FROM "MADE IN CHINA" TO "MADE BY CHINA"

The famous saying of Stan Shih, founder of the Taiwanese computer maker Acer and a businessman of mythic proportion, " 'Me too' is not my style" has become the new slogan.[7] The perpetual low-end offer has largely disappeared from these Chinese groups' offer. Today some appliance, telephonic infrastructure, and industrial pumps coming from China are qualitatively very close to the leading products of rival multinationals—but are sold at lower prices. For most central purchasing departments, the pressure is strong to accede to a first, tempting offer from a Chinese company. The fishing experiment, if successful, can then be transformed into a more solid partnership between buyer and seller, which eventually may lead to collaborations in research and development. Thus Huawei declares it runs a dozen centers for innovation in common with the operators of telecommunications companies, especially in Europe.

All major Chinese firms owe their success partly to close collaboration with Chinese administrations, national or regional, that in one way or another are interested in their success. The advantages include favorable tax treatment and diplomatic assistance, in particular for investments outside the core business. Here the "referring elevator" is commonplace, in China just as elsewhere in the world.

STRUCTURAL WEAKNESSES—MIRROR OF THE THREE STRENGTHS

Chinese groups are still very oriented to the internal market, and so the internationalized corporations remain the exception (although the new positioning of Xi Jinping's "China within Asia" might change the situation). In contradistinction to Western, Japanese, or Korean multinationals, which generate 80 to 90 percent of their revenue outside their borders, all Chinese groups (except for Geely-

Volvo) that are implanted in Europe exhibit an inverse proportion: at most 10 percent of their sales originate abroad. Only three of them—Lenovo, thanks to its purchase of IBM assets; Geely, through automobile shares; and Huawei—have a European coverage that is almost complete.

The one-man show of Chinese moguls illustrates the limits of governance Chinese style. A close look shows that the majority of managers and administrators are not in the right position with regard to their competence. On the other hand, they are often intimately linked to the boss (through family relationships or long friendships), and so they cannot express critical opinions. The Confucian system does not help. Managerial bodies do exist but are often fictive, since decisions are made in private conversations, often with the help of obscure advisers. Between the two poles of decision making (solo, by a "big man," or anonymous, behind a curtain), hybrid or opaque systems of governance are erected: the head of Huawei, Ren Zhengfei, seventy years old, unsuccessfully formed a triumvirate consisting of Eric Li, Guo Ping, and Ken Hu to direct the group alongside him, although it was widely understood that the company would remain within the family. The children of the founder are already inside the organization, starting with Ren's daughter, Cathy Meng, the Huawei Group's CFO. Despite efforts at communication and "transparency in this company, a great opacity persists, akin to the situation at ChemChina-BlueStar, where foreign experts are merely advisers in charge of transferring skills.

Still more anachronistic is the very structure of the groups in question. The Chinese norm is an amalgam of companies interwoven with each other, with several of them quoted on the stock exchange and the motherhouse almost invisible. With the exception of Japanese businesses, a good number of Asian family multinational corporations and groups operate in a similar way, but rarely to such a degree. SOEs are even more complex, since they are closely interlinked with political power, sometimes even with the army and security services. As for Huawei, it is not listed on the stock exchange and will perhaps never be, given its origins (complex, at the very least), linked to the Chinese military.

In the medium or long term, the question of succession will certainly force these groups to modify their governance in order to avoid an implosion or a cumbersome restructuring. During a grand assembly of investment fund managers in Hong Kong in 2014, some people asked whether it would soon be possible to acquire 100 percent of the subsidiaries of these Chinese empires by skillfully negotiating with the second generation of directors, for the latter aim more at profitability and tranquility than at frenetically pursuing world growth.

Edging toward a Policy of Innovation

It is difficult to position oneself as a global actor without at one time or another demonstrating a desire to innovate. "Innovation" was even the keyword at the Chinese version of the World Economic Forum in Dalian in September 2013. But to date, investments are tardy, and the Chinese are far from the Japanese and Korean models.

The Chinese corporations cannot be reproached for giving priority to mastering the technologies of tomorrow. But there is no durable revolution in this respect. Research and development centers flourish here and there (such as the Swedish center China Euro Vehicle Technology AB, co-financed by Geely and its subsidiary, Volvo, which has more than 200 employees, a majority of whom are Chinese), and partnerships are formed with universities, although concrete results are not yet forthcoming. Should Westerners risk a comparison with the research centers of their own multinational corporations in China? This issue also leads to questions about secrecy and the theft of intellectual property.

Autonomy and Fair Play

Chinese mutual aid networks, whether they are political, familial, or regional, generally procure for their beneficiaries a certain degree of autonomy (as long as it not a one-way street). But a strength on the domestic market may turn out to be a handicap on international markets. Many major Chinese groups have had difficulties managing their own interests in international competition, where the operating rules are the same for all. Political or direct stakes are also handicaps that engender irrationalities in the choice, the price, or the size of investments. For example, it is recognized that ChemChina did not apply its usual rigor and independence in the course of its three great acquisitions in Europe, and the mood of its legendary CEO cannot explain everything. Similarly, the difficulties Zoomlion experienced in producing a solid sheaf of orders for its own equipment in Italy are no doubt partly linked to its lack of comprehension of the rules of allocating contracts in Europe. Yet the latter are less random and less opaque than China's.

THREE CHALLENGES FOR CHINESE INVESTORS IN EUROPE

In this section, we look at the main practical challenges for Chinese companies while they are trying to make headway in the European market.

1. Lack of Truly Original Products

No multinational has ever succeeded without ensuring the presence of its brands on the international market, most often in the form of products that are immediately recognizable and distinct. Chinese groups are still far off the mark. Lenovo, the best-established enterprise internationally, sells principally portable computers from IBM's old personal computer unit, which Lenovo bought in 2004, and is trying to enter the server business. ChemChina, like Geely and Sany, have acquired nice nuggets, but without appropriating a savoir faire that is unique in the world. Haier and Huawei pursue their rise upmarket but are still far from selling top-of-the-line items.

To protect itself, China has long imposed restrictive standards on foreign firms in many strategic sectors. In this way it has propelled its national market leaders into the international field, but then prevented them from drawing a profit from their leading products, which are not adapted to international markets.

2. The Brand Deficit

The brand name today is an integral part of any evaluation and professional valorization of a multinational; its value can be worth billions of euros. According to a mid-2014 analysis by Millward Brown, a market research company with a global reputation, Chinese enterprises suffer from a brand recognition deficit. Nine of them are among the hundred most important brands in the world, yet even the best recognized ranks only fifteenth, and among the nine brands, there is not a single one of the Chinese industrial giants that are implanted in Europe.[8] A study done in Germany at the end of 2013 by Globeone, a local marketing firm, confirms this scenario: barely 17 percent of respondents questioned (out of a panel of 1,000 local consumers) could recognize a single Chinese brand.[9]

The legitimate decision to retain the names of brands acquired during an investment takeover (for example, Putzmeister in Germany, Volvo in Sweden) does not favor better advertising. But there is a real concern for legitimacy and recognition for names like Lenovo, Huawei (whose logo strangely resembles that of a major American TV network), or Haier (whose spoken name sounds like the second half of its early German partner, Liebherr). COSCO, COMAC, and AVIC have no international name recognition whatsoever.

3. An Imperfect Union of Developed and Emerging Countries

To satisfy the criterion of a multinational corporation with global spread requires a double dynamic that serves both Western developed countries and a substantial number of emerging countries. This is still far from the case for the majority of Chinese firms with a presence in Europe. Wanda, for example, despite its impressive acquisitions in the United States and the United Kingdom, remains relatively unknown in the rest of the world. No doubt the absence of Chinese personnel who are truly international and ready to expatriate is a sizable handicap for this development.

THE RISKS OF MAINTAINING THE STATUS QUO FOR CHINESE MULTINATIONAL CORPORATIONS

For Chinese companies, the challenges are great when it comes to adapting their management style to a European business environment.

1. A Largely Monocultural Management

It seems clear that Chinese business moguls are not prepared to share power with newcomers, and even less inclined to do so with foreigners. With rare exceptions, such as Lenovo, non-Chinese employees never benefit from real confidence from management. Language is obviously an obstacle, but it cannot explain or justify everything. International prominence necessitates an intercultural approach that Chinese enterprises do not seem ready to adopt.

2. Overlooking Organic Growth in Favor of Continued External Growth

It is not enough to execute even significant acquisitions in order to expand beyond natural frontiers; one still has to envisage the future beyond organic growth. Two of the groups we studied in this book, Haier and Huawei, already comfortably dominate the Chinese market in their sectors. But are they capable of realizing important acquisitions outside their frontiers? Nothing is less sure; however, management scholars generally recommend that firms interested in growth take the initiative so as not to run out of steam. On the other hand, firms like Geely or ChemChina that have increasing outbound investments may run the risk of not being able to finance the follow-up phases.

3. Diversification Can Be Overdone

Recent research shows that diversification is often a trap, even if financial merits can be recognized in this approach. In Japan, Korea, and Singapore, any self-respecting group is a conglomerate with multiple activities. On the Chinese side, two tendencies stand out: specializing, such as done by Haier, Huawei, Lenovo, or Sany, and diversifying, as done by Fosun and Wanda.

By the end of 2015, when Chinese groups were multiplying their incursions into European territory, it was still too early to assess the outcome, but the almost systematic preference for diversification over specialization might be worrying with respect to the difficulties that Chinese groups have in adapting to the international field. Moreover, the Chinese partiality toward speculative decisions made on the fly is well known.

As an example, the current Chinese champion of internationalization is based in Hong Kong—Li Ka-shing's business empire—and distinguishes itself through two activities, which it has consolidated over twenty years in its two venerable companies, Hutchison Whampoa and Cheung Kong Holdings: managing port infrastructures and managing commercial infrastructures.

4. The Stranglehold of State-Owned Enterprises

For more than fifteen years, Chinese SOEs have been subject to the imperatives of surviving the competition and turning a profit, with the principal objective of creating (thirty-some) national and international industry leaders capable of rivaling the best in the world. For a long time this vast and ambitious mission was mired in oblivion or else did not benefit from any practical measures, which, when they were undertaken, were more often symbolic and superficial than benefit producing.

Suddenly, in 2015—no doubt in the face of declining growth, and under sustained pressure from the authorities to give substance to the image of a China that is stronger internationally—a real change finally came, which took two principal forms, mergers and consolidation of the largest SOEs.

In the space of a few months, SOEs in sectors as strategic as rail and nuclear energy were forced to merge, in an effort to curb their often derisory competition with each other and to set up a coherent and much more solid organization in the face of the world's giants. China Southern Railway and China Northern Railways merged at the start of 2015, becoming China Railway Rolling, a formidable competitor of Siemens AG or Alstom SA. Then China Power Investment Corporation and the State Nuclear Power Technology Corporation did the same in the summer of 2015 to form the State Power Investment Corporation. The merger of the top two companies in the sector, China National Nuclear Corporation and China General Nuclear Power Group, is under consideration.

Rumors are also circulating about restructuring the petroleum and petrochemical sectors in one way or another. Integrating Sinochem and China National Offshore Oil Corporation and/or PetroChina into Sinopec would trigger an unprecedented upheaval and would redistribute the pieces on the global chessboard.

As an important signal, the state-owned Assets Supervision and Administration Commission of the State Council (SASAC) confirmed in September 2015 the endorsement of a large-scale plan titled "Instructions on Deepening Reforms of State-Owned Enterprises."[10]

The joint venture announced in May 2015 between the China Investment Corporation (CIC) and the China National Cereals, Oils and Foodstuffs Corporation (COFCO) gave birth to a formidable world platform in primary foodstuffs.[11] It followed on the heels of sustained acquisitions by COFCO in the four corners of the world and enabled COFCO (with the financial support of the all-powerful CIC) to sit at the table with the biggest players in the field, Archer

Daniels Midland, Bunge, Cargill, and Louis Dreyfus—the "ABCDs" of global agribusiness.

Each of these initiatives made sense, and was even innovative, but they left no place for private entrepreneurs—quite the contrary, in the cases of COFCO and ChemChina. The actions of these SOEs resulted in an even greater stranglehold on private companies by the highest level of the Chinese bureaucracy.

FOUR

GREAT STRETCHES IN CHINESE FINANCE

In the heady days of the World Cup soccer games in June 2014, which saw France advancing to the quarter-finals, Paris enjoyed an unexpected victory: the announcement of the purchase of the five-star Marriott Hotel on the famous Champs-Élysées by a Chinese group for €350 million. After the partnership of convenience signed by the French energy company GDF Suez (now Engie) and the Chinese sovereign fund, the China Investment Corporation (CIC), in the summer of 2011 (the agreement gave China a 30 percent stake in the French company's non-strategic gas and oil exploration and production business), this was the first transaction worthy of the name in France.[1] It was understood in advance to be a logical investment: Chinese tourists stream en masse into the French capital, amounting to 2 million visitors in 2014, and the Chinese government promotes tourism as a way to encourage consumers to spend money.

Opinion on this transaction must be reserved, however, because the buyer, Kai Yuan Holdings, is an illustrious unknown that manages a minuscule turnover of €75 million, with a loss of €10 million in 2013. It had to borrow €206 million ($280 million) from one of its shareholders, divesting 5.54 percent of its shares to finance the acquisition of the hotel. Fortunately, the company is owned by a relative of China's former top leader Hu Jintao. As this information was quietly made public, the share value rose 60 percent in a few days on the Hong Kong Stock Exchange, whereas the figures indicated at the start might have made the stock price fall (that is, the stock price rose not on the basis of fundamentals but because of the relationship of Kai Yuan Holdings to the top tier of the PRC's political system).

This anecdote is entirely consistent with the image of the Chinese entrepreneurial world, with its nebulous and irrational aspects, on glimpsing which observers are taken aback. For thirty years these situations have only multiplied, which obliges one to raise—in a nuanced way, since there is no obligation to be transparent in mergers and acquisitions unless acquirers are listed on the stock exchange—some technical questions.

HOW RATIONAL ARE THE VALUATIONS AND PURCHASE PRICES OF CHINESE ACQUISITIONS?

Transactions must make sense in terms of the price paid, since a deal (or a succession of deals) that is priced too high would pose serious risks to profitability, even solvency. The petroleum sector is illustrative, since it is by far the most actively pursued sector in Chinese international purchases, accounting for almost €100 billion spent on acquisitions. After being in a state of permanent effervescence for more than ten years (2004–13), movement in the sector halted abruptly in the spring of 2014 under the aegis of a more rigorous policy, with the Chinese authorities implying that the prosperous period of growth in assets should give way to a different mode, one valorizing certain key terms, such as "return on investment" and "budgetary discipline."

The rules governing mergers and acquisitions are many and varied. However, they still must adhere to a few principles, three of which are linked to developing an appropriate ratio of price to the value of the target company: (1) the valuation multiples applicable to sectors and conjunctures should be aligned; (2) the target company's drivers of growth should be identified, to support any possible overvaluation; and (3) there must be a coherent size match: the investor's acquisitive appetite should be trimmed to its own set of skills, resources, and competencies. When evaluated by their performance in relation to these three principles, the large Chinese investments in Europe form an eclectic mosaic, running from the very formulaic to the very exotic, from the highly profitable deal to the one that could be called a fiasco. The norm is found in most of the acquisitions of groups like Sany and Zoomlion: the valuation multiples are in line with the market, the engines of growth are well identified, and the logic of appropriate size is respected.

The logic of valuation is less evident in the automobile industry. In 2014, PSA Peugeot-Citroën offered on a sacrificial platter 14 percent of its capital to its Chinese competitor, Dongfeng Motor Corporation, valuing any vehicle manufactured at barely €1,000 (by contrast, Volkswagen vehicles were valued at fifteen times more than what Dongfeng paid to buy PSA). The situation was quite the opposite for the Zhejiang Geely Holding Group when it moved to acquire the Swedish company Volvo Cars from Ford Motor Company in 2010: it paid only €4,000 per car, but invested in an enterprise crippled with debt and did so without market reference points, as at that time, few car companies were sold or acquired. What is more, it proposed a recovery plan of €8 billion, bringing the total cost to almost €10 billion, although it did not produce more cars than Volvo and had a war chest of only hundreds of millions of dollars at most. What financed this headlong rush to acquire automotive companies? The answer lies partly in how Chinese companies are financed.

Other industrial sectors exhibit a spectrum of acquisition prices. The Shanghai conglomerate Fosun has the reputation of paying a fair price, as do a number of its counterparts in the luxury market. However, this is less often the case in vineyard transactions, where prices have sometimes bordered on the ridiculous. Maotai, the unquestioned leader of liquor distilling in China, was reported to depend heavily on the firm's legal adviser, who apparently knew more than the company did about Bordeaux estate valuations.

HOW ARE CHINESE COMPANIES FINANCED?

The second question concerns the financing (properly speaking) of these projects. Do Chinese companies manage to do in Europe what they do so well everywhere else, taking advantage of the tailor-made assistance from Chinese banks, which sometimes lend unreasonable sums at rates that would be infeasible to the competition? The indebtedness of Latin American countries to China, a situation systematically put in place through Chinese-built projects, exceeded $100 billion for the period 2005–13.

There is one striking constant about the practices of Chinese financing at the international level and in Europe in particular: the very weak contribution in capital per se, and consequently the immense dependence on third-party loans. In the West, beyond the transactions that are under the control of investment funds, such a disequilibrium is not at all the norm. It is obviously possible to accept an accounting explanation of this preference for indebtedness, since using one's own funds is the most costly means of financing. However, such an explanation masks weaknesses, both macroeconomic and specific to the enterprises in question. On the one hand, there is a certain "amateurism" evident in the Chinese and Hong Kong stock exchanges, which do not have the capacity or the will to facilitate the issuing of new stocks related to the acquisition of companies outside their region. On the other hand, acquiring firms often exhibit a narrow outlook and amateurism of their own in failing, for example, to set up a stock swap or exchange with the targeted companies. Finally, any contribution to financing in the form of a war chest—profits amassed over time and set aside for later use—is markedly insufficient for many of these giant corporations in full expansion mode.

Indebtedness, which should be only one among many options, thus becomes an obligation. What is more, the road to forced borrowing is strewn with pitfalls. The renminbi (RMB)-denominated obligations markets in China or abroad, a thousand times promised a fine future, are still in their infancy.

That leaves only one alternative, to get financing from either Chinese or foreign banks. Here too the path gets narrower and steeper: few or no Japanese, American, or European banks seem to be heavily involved in financing Chinese mergers and acquisitions. The conquest of the West is occurring thanks to Chinese financial institutions alone. The billion euros necessary for Fosun's purchase of the Portuguese insurance company Caixa Geral de Depósitos was guaranteed in part by €550 million loaned by the Industrial and Commercial Bank of China (ICBC), the largest bank in the country. Huawei's deficit abroad exceeds €3 billion on the books of the China Development Bank (CDB). Similarly, the deficit abroad of COFCO (China National Cereals, Oils and Foodstuffs Corporation), a state-owned and almost monopolistic company, enabled it to acquire for a little less than €1 billion 51 percent of the Dutch grain trading company Nidera BV at the start of 2014. Nidera has been active all over the world since its origin at the start of the twentieth century. The billions needed for Geely to purchase and recover Volvo assets came from loans contracted with three other financial actors, the Bank of China (BOC), the China Construction Bank (CCB), and the Export-Import Bank of China (China Exim Bank), in addition to money lent by various provincial or local institutions. The acquisition of CIFA (Compagnia Italiana Forme Acciaio) by Zoomlion was conditioned on six loans of various kinds from

four institutions. Outside China, such massive largesse had never
been seen.

HOW DO LARGE CHINESE BANKS WORK
WITH CHINESE INVESTORS?

The whole edifice of expansion beyond Chinese borders is connected above all to the role played by the CDB, the largest development bank in the world. Without the CDB, no significant project
would ever see the light of day, starting with the enormous infrastructure projects such as the Three Gorges Dam on the Yangtze
River. Founded in 1994, the CDB depends directly on central government funding and therefore offers an infallible guarantee, which
allows it to set up financing on conditions much better than those
offered by its competitors. Since 2007 the threat of seeing its status
as a privileged development institution withdrawn has hung over
the CDB, on the correct assumption that its position and activities
are damaging the viability of all other domestic commercial banks,
which depend on markets and interest rates to provide financing to
borrowers.

Internationally, the CDB works with almost 140 nations or private partners, for an outstanding loan amount exceeding €200 billion. Its portfolio of loans is unlimited in size and its credit lines are
unheard of. Thus it lends colossal sums to clients such as Huawei in
the form of trade financing, thereby facilitating the expansion plans
and market share increase of this telecom giant. This practice, which
is commonplace in China, is very rare in the West.

The CDB also lends important sums in the form of open credit,
leaving the way open to third-party loans (in which the initial loan
is used as a guarantee). Again, this is a current practice in China
that is found much less frequently in Europe. Finally, the CDB fi-
nances various development funds in various parts of the world, of
which two are specific to Europe: the Sino-Italian fund Mandarin

Capital Partners and the Sino-Belgian Fund, the latter of which invested in moving a chocolate factory from Flanders to Suzhou.

Above all, the sponsorship of the CDB is political and financial, being intimately tied to the government's long-term ambitions,[2] and is quite evidently maintained by very close relations among the state, the bank, and investors. As a function of connections between the banks and the borrowing company, a commercial dynamic is put in place, often hewing to the typical schema of a lead bank followed by a few others, a sort of equitable dividing up of the cake.

In general, rational criteria for bank lending are indeed present, but they come into play after other sorts of criteria are satisfied. The interest rates are usually in line with the market, but the volume of money borrowed frequently is above the threshold of prudence. In addition, the largesse of the lending bodies in renewing a debt or partially discounting it induces risks that few Western banks would assume.

Probably overstretched (though no proven cause-and-effect link is known), the CDB, the ICBC, and other Chinese banks have significantly trimmed their sails recently. The CDB, for example, did not participate in the largest transaction of 2014, the acquisition by Shanghui Corporation, the biggest pork producer in China, of its rival, the American firm Smithfield Foods, for $4.7 billion. And the ICBC was severely burned by the latest report of the National Audit Service—a sort of accounting office for major state companies—in June 2014: no less than €6 billion in loans were not properly justified.

COULD THIS MONEY BE LAUNDERED OR STASHED IN TAX HAVENS?

Are the transactions structured according to the usual models, or do the firms hope to escape oversight and taxes? Many observers compare China and its explosion of wealth and billionaires with

Russia and its oligarchs, who often maneuver using unorthodox practices.

In this respect, an assessment of China ultimately shows few shadow zones, at least as far as the business dealings of large corporations are concerned. The provenance of funds is identifiable and the financial and tax structuring model is rather classic, with the creation of special vehicles in places like Hong Kong and Luxembourg or Monaco in order to optimize the fiscal regimes. Any Western project of the same sort and magnitude would follow very similar standards.

However, strong presumptions of money laundering do arise in relation to certain small-scale operations, as remarked by an official at Tracfin, the unit of the French Ministry of Finance fighting money laundering, who noted possible misappropriations or embezzlements in the acquisition of vineyards by foreign investors, including Chinese investors, and called for vigilance. Red flags had been raised by the large number of shell corporations and by the frequent changes in ownership, often in record time. These variants were also noted in the above-mentioned report of the Chinese National Audit Service.

HOW CRITICAL IS THE ROLE OF SOVEREIGN AND PRIVATE EQUITY?

Is the 30 percent equity investment of the CIC in a subsidiary of French utility giant Engie the norm or the exception for the biggest Chinese sovereign fund? What added values and possible trade-offs are in play in owning such a large stake of a foreign corporation?

From tradition to innovation: that is the trajectory of state-fund operations, whether conventional or tailor-made.

Lurking in the shadows, the CIC is undoubtedly if surprisingly the most important investor in Europe. Close to 22 percent of its share portfolio consists of European shares, acquired principally through low-percentage participation in the largest multinational corporations on the European continent. These are predominantly passive and low-risk investments, very much aligned with what sovereign funds like those in the Middle East would do. In the same spirit of searching for stable and recurring profits, the CIC is also heavily invested in the infrastructure sector, with no less than €2 billion disbursed in 2012–13. Its investments in this sector include ownership of 10 percent of the shares in London's Heathrow Airport and a little less than 9 percent of the shares in Thames Water Corporation, the British leader in water treatment. A logical light sectorial diversification aimed at slightly better returns has been achieved with a 7 percent participation in the capital of Eutelsat, a French satellite provider of global size. That Bpifrance (formerly the French Strategic Investment Fund; "Bpi" stands for La Banque publique d'investissement) holds 25 percent of Eutelsat's capital certainly proved an attractant for the Chinese, whetting their appetite for sitting at the same table as other reputable and renowned global institutional actors.

In the same vein of investment without much drama or fuss, we note the recent operation by the People's Bank of China—China's central bank—which acquired slightly over 2 percent of the capital of two Italian energy groups, Eni and Enel. These acquisitions represented investments of €1.3 billion and €800 million, respectively.

At the opposite end of the spectrum, the active involvement of the largest private capital funds, both Chinese and foreign, is key in many leading instances of the Chinese assault on the European market. From Goldman Sachs to Barings, from Blackstone to KKR, from Hopu to Hony Capital, almost all the private debt and equity giants in the United States, Europe, and China are implicated in most of the largest transactions made by the multinational corporations that are most strongly rooted in Europe—the likes of Zoomlion, COFCO, Haier, and ChemChina-BlueStar.

The story of the triumvirate orchestrating the purchase of CIFA by Zoomlion is exemplary in many respects. It began in 2005 and culminated in 2013, nine years into the partnership, with five principal episodes.

Act one began in December 2005, when Hony Capital signed an agreement to assume a 16 percent participation in Zoomlion. In fact, this was a handshake agreement between two heavyweights: Hony's boss, John Zhao, and the CEO of Zoomlion, Zhan Chunxin. John Zhao had built Hony Capital from scratch. Beginning in 2003 as a small independent unit within Legend-Lenovo dedicated to the management of third-party finance projects for the group, it gradually became the largest private investment fund in China over three years, still with Lenovo as the core shareholder, together with pension funds and "family offices" from across the entire world. Its ambition was to take minority ownership positions in up-and-coming Chinese enterprises and to make inroads and money by accelerating their development, as well as by improving their performance.

Zhan Chunxin got the message. A few years earlier he had taken the reins of Zoomlion, a former state company, profiting from the economic boom but still managing it conservatively in the old Chinese way, confining business to its home province of Hunan, in the center of China.

The second act took place in 2008, after two years of collaboration that had proved fruitful beyond expectations. Zoomlion had doubled in size and quintupled its profits, and its quotation on the stock exchange had increased by 700 percent. It now had relatively solid control of the domestic market and was seeking to internationalize. Concomitantly a rumor circulated from Italy that Magenta, the Milanese family fund that owned CIFA, might be ready to sell the enterprise, and the perennial rival of Zoomlion, Sany Construction, was on the rails. The price tag was €500 million, an amount that neither Hony nor Zoomlion could raise or easily invest on its own. Nor did they have privileged ties with Italy or with its banks—and still less with CIFA.

The third episode occurred a few months later, when a quartet of entities bought up the entirety of CIFA: Zoomlion took 60 percent, while Hony and two other funds, Goldman Sachs and Mandarin Capital Partners, shared the remaining 40 percent equally. Goldman Sachs put on the table its outsized reputation associated with its premier expertise in complex cross-border mergers and acquisitions. Mandarin Capital Partners brought the relational aspect, the domestic touch, and facilitated getting the blessing and approbation of the Chinese authorities, in particular the approval of the mastermind of China's National Development and Reform Commission (NDRC), the super-ministry charged with supervising reforms and major economic operations in Beijing. Created in 2005 by two Italian businessmen and supported by renowned Chinese and Italian institutions (including the China Exim Bank, the CDB, and the Intesa Sanpaolo Bank), Mandarin Capital focused solely on opportunities to get companies from the two countries together. In line with this mission, it conducted a brilliant public relations campaign to rally any major member of the Milanese (and Chinese) establishment to its cause.

The fourth act spanned the five years of Zoomlion's and CIFA's life together, which saw both high points, such as getting listed on the Hong Kong Stock Exchange at the end of 2013, and low points, such as facing charges of accounting irregularities, principally the artificial inflation of client debt. The fifth and final act was the planned exit at the start of 2013, with Zoomlion buying up the 40 percent share from the three other shareholders according to an arrangement fixed contractually at the start.

In the end, each party fulfilled its role and kept its engagements. Zoomlion would never have been able to acquire and then integrate CIFA without the assistance of these investments funds, but, on the other hand, it had to pay the market price.

If a combination of opportunistic moves and favorable circumstances smiled on these four protagonists, the same cannot be said about all such transactions. The U.S. private equity firm Carlyle, having invested $200 million in the appliance group Haier in 2011 and getting one of nine board seats, quietly sold its position back four years later, taking advantage of a substantial capital gain resulting from a spectacular jump in Haier's stock price. The rationale for such a price increase can be linked to overall stock exchange reasons and not to any value added such a reputable private equity fund is supposed to bring, and very often publicizes at the time of exit.[3] For its part, Blackstone, a 20 percent stakeholder in ChemChina-BlueStar for $600 million since 2008, by 2015 was desperately seeking an amicable exit.

In part, such divestments reflect a change in the funding picture from what had obtained ten years earlier. Many huge Chinese companies today seem better equipped and opt to venture out alone, or, if accompanied by investment partners, then strictly by Chinese funds.

Another facet of capital funds is the rarity of entities of more modest size, such as Cathay Capital, that have a mandate to construct economic bridges between European and Chinese small and medium-sized businesses. Cathay Capital was created in 2007 and continues to be directed by its founders. With offices in Paris, Shanghai, Beijing, and New York, in 2014 Cathay managed two funds of more than €600 million earmarked to be invested in France, China, and Germany, in particular under the protection of two principal backers, the CDB and Bpifrance. Both funds operate through "sweet spot" investments, in amounts ranging between €15 and €50 million, in Entreprises de Taille Intermédiaire (ETIs, mid-sized businesses) in the sectors of health and clean technology, as well as in various other industries, with the ambition of creating a triangular synergy among the three countries. As of late 2014, €150 million had been invested without leading to the creation of a new small Chinese leader in any of the industries of interest. The energy is not lacking, nor is the uncontested talent of Cai Ming-Po, president, managing director, and cofounder of Cathay Capital, in question, but there are difficulties of execution and in the discovery of the rare nugget.[4]

WHAT IS THE RELATIONSHIP
BETWEEN CHINESE BANKS AND THE
INTERNATIONALIZATION OF THE YUAN?

The last line of questioning concerns the position of Chinese banks, from London to Frankfurt by way of Paris and Luxembourg. In 2014 alone, China's central government suddenly granted ten authorizations to banks to develop their businesses in Europe. Why?

Despite the opening of branch offices, Chinese banks are still rather quiet in Europe, even though they are the biggest in the world in terms of assets, and among the most profitable. Their position owes to their profitable and closed-up domestic market and their self-confidence; in this respect they are very much like their Japanese counterparts, which similarly did not collapse during the 2008–09 financial crisis.

In relation to the massive stakes, the four tenors in the sector—the ICBC, the BOC, the CCB, and Agricultural Bank of China (ABC)—still claim only modest staffing and presence in the key financial centers of London, Frankfurt, Luxembourg, and Paris, and in the next tier cities of Brussels, Madrid, and Milan. Their activities are extremely small scale in all major traditional banking activities, such as playing a brokering role in exchange rates and in stocks and liabilities, as well as roles in private and investment banking. In fact, they are most influential and most noticeably present in the single sector where their positioning procures them a decisive advantage, commercial lending. They are devoted to two well-targeted segments: first, European multinational corporations that are trying to develop in China and are looking for alternative local financing, where the large Chinese banks are an indispensable part of extending lending facilities beyond what Western banks would typically lend; and second, the large number of enterprises in the public works sector or infrastructure that are experiencing difficulty getting financing from European banks alone.

Chinese financial institutions profit sufficiently from this inflow from two major market segments to maintain a presence in the European capitals of finance. In Greece alone in the spring of 2014, more than €5 billion in credits were set up to support local companies involved in vast harbor, hydroelectric, and wind power projects. In the United Kingdom, ICBC also loaned almost €1 billion to groups charged with renovating and enlarging the Manchester Airport.

The Chinese institutions working in these markets are not particularly exuberant in making acquisitions. Only ICBC has taken the plunge, indirectly, through two small transactions. At the end of 2013, it bought for €600 million a 60 percent stake in the London subsidiary specializing in the exchange rate sector of a mid-sized South African institution, Standard Bank, in which ICBC had held a 20 percent stake since 2008. And in April 2014, ICBC took control (a 76 percent stake) of a Turkish textile bank, Tekstilbank, for €250 million.[5]

This reticence can be partly explained by the structure of Chinese banking. Chinese banks realize 95 percent of their activity and their profits inside China, competing in a highly complex market whose development is still subject to the vagaries of the central and local authorities that sponsor the banks as much as they supervise them. This framework curbs the appearance of full competition, often by privileging relationship-based banking success over an approach that gives priority to services and expertise. Once in the West, and left somewhat to their own devices, Chinese bankers are critically devoid of address books and lacking in technical skills. In the business arena and banking circles of most European countries, Chinese brands and ensigns are still far from being recognized. Incidentally, in the financial sector, reciprocity is the rule; as we have seen, China is far from practicing free competition in its market (foreign banks know a lot about this situation).

Certain recent events, however, offer a glimpse of a more significant presence of Chinese banks in Europe. Since the start of 2014, an unprecedented battle has raged among the four major Chinese commercial banks, as well as among the four financial centers of choice—London, Frankfurt, Paris, and Luxembourg. The stakes are enormous and justify frenetic lobbying campaigns, shock announcements, and costly forums. The principle at stake is how to profit most quickly and abundantly from the internationalization of the Chinese currency, the renminbi (RMB), which will open up huge potential, and under accelerating conditions. London seems clearly in the lead. In 2013, China accounted for almost 15 percent of world GDP and 10 percent of world trade, and for more than 5 percent of global investments, but its currency accounted for barely 1 percent of all these exchanges. This percentage enabled it, however, to reach the number ten spot among the most utilized currencies at the international level, whereas it had ranked only twentieth a few years earlier.

Another stunning ascent is in the domain of shares and bonds. For example, the market for "dim-sum bonds,"[6] bonds that are denominated in RMB outside China, did not even exist in 2010 but was expected to exceed issuance of $65 billion in 2014 (a figure revised downward to $23 billion issuance by October 2015).[7] As for the quotas for buying Chinese stocks in Chinese currency (the Renminbi Qualified Foreign Institutional Investor program), they have increased spectacularly, from €2.5 billion in 2010 to more than €40 billion in 2014.[8] Moreover, they can now be offered to a larger panel of nations and financial institutions of all kinds, including hedge funds. China notched an additional economic milestone in late November 2015, with the International Monetary Fund adding the renminbi to its elite basket of reserve currencies, a move designed to spur greater liberalization in the world's number two economy.[9]

Among the myriad agreements concluded and commitments made in recent years that exemplify these phenomena, three are of special note. First, authorization was given to the central banks of the countries of the four European financial centers to collaborate officially with their Chinese counterpart, the People's Bank of China, to establish in timely fashion local financial centers for the renminbi, covering both compensation and settlement in Chinese currency. Second, in London, the CCB became the first Chinese bank authorized to perform the above-mentioned operations in renminbi, while negotiations are under way to upgrade its status from a representative office to a branch. Such a change is fundamental, since it permits offering a complete range of all classic banking activities, which the CCB was not able to take advantage of previously. Third is the execution, in March 2014, through the BOC in Luxembourg of the very first loan in renminbi by a Chinese firm, for the significant amount of €300 million. Until then, all renminbi-denominated borrowings involved foreign banks.[10]

It is too soon to draw any conclusions from these tentative beginnings, but the battle between these various banking and financial center protagonists likely will only intensify over the coming years, as will the profit those activities could generate. As of now the CCB has taken an unexpected lead, whereas observers were wagering on the BOC or ICBC. Less surprising is the progress made by London and Luxembourg as they pull ahead of Paris and Frankfurt.[11] No doubt they are counting on keeping this lead, since London deals with 60 percent of the transactions in renminbi outside China (and Hong Kong), while Luxembourg has become the preferred financial location for Chinese banks. Welcomed with open arms by the government of the Grand Duchy, all of them have established their European headquarters there.[12]

These banking and financial dealings are also eminently political and are the subject of negotiations at the highest official level between those countries, with China best practicing its favorite game, dividing to conquer, and being careful never to give the advantage to any single bank or financial center.[13] This is the recipe it has successfully applied for thirty years.

FIVE

THE CHALLENGES OF ACCULTURATION

In business, it is legitimate to ask whether Europeans make accommodations for Beijing's "authoritarian consensus." Previously, cultural problems were not impediments to a significant rapprochement between Chinese and European business people, especially in the domain of mergers and acquisitions. Yet despite the arrival of a generation of Chinese who have been trained abroad, mutual trust has not yet been achieved. It will take time.

THE HISTORIC EAST-WEST ENCOUNTER

For more than forty years now, Chinese and Westerners have been seeing a lot of each other in the economic sphere. Beginning at the end of the 1970s, a first generation of European enterprises traveled the road to Beijing to meet the teams put in place after Deng Xiaoping's return to power in 1978. Groups like EDF, Framatome (which later became Areva), Alstom, Volkswagen, Philips, and Danone entered into major negotiations, some of which turned out successfully, others of which were beset with difficulties and led to surprising discoveries or unexpected demands. At the start of the 1980s, one participant recalled, the fashion designer and businessman Pierre Cardin was invited to Beijing to meet Deng, hoping to get the green light to establish stores. To his great surprise, the "little helmsman" asked him to launch a Maxim's-style restaurant, like the one he had just bought on the rue Royale in Paris.[1]

Everyone who worked in China in the 1980s got to know the spartan, even glacial ambience there. The negotiations, punctuated with cups of tea and cigarette smoke, took place in rooms furnished with a large negotiating table, on one side of which sat a group of Western businessmen, accompanied by their interpreter and possibly an intermediary, very often a Chinese aide from Hong Kong or the Chinese diaspora. On the other side sat an official Chinese delegation, most of the time not very talkative, yet prompt to adjourn to a neighboring room for consultation as soon as a question appeared too arduous or politically incorrect (which apparently it was about half the time). When the negotiations took place in China, they were "supervised" by the Chinese party in terms of the agenda, which was often modified at the last minute, and the program included many banquets, karaoke sessions, and visits to tourist sites, all intended to foster harmonious relations. Quite often the solution to the "problem," if there was one, appeared between the lines of a conversation otherwise peppered with mundane and general commentary.

Abroad, the ambiance was more relaxed—the European hosts knew how to do such things—but another problem often arose: there was no question of the Chinese making a quick decision without consulting Beijing. The hesitancy to say anything conclusive was exacerbated by an atmosphere of distrust among members of the delegation, for in that era requests for asylum abroad were not rare. A dialogue of the deaf frequently ensued: the Westerners considered a complete dossier sufficient ground on which to make a decision, while for the Chinese negotiators, trust was a decisive factor in negotiations, and spending long days together was essential to reaching a decision. Once confidence was established, the actual negotiation became almost secondary.

James Mann, former Beijing bureau chief for the *Los Angeles Times* and the author of the memorable book, *Beijing Jeep* (1989), on one of the first joint ventures ever negotiated between Westerners and representatives of the People's Republic of China, described the 1981 negotiations around Beijing Jeep this way:

> The talks took place in a Spartan conference room at the Chinese jeep factory. . . . Preparing or distributing any kind of written material proved difficult because the Chinese factory had no photocopying machine. . . . Sometimes, [we] would watch while Chinese negotiators asked their aides to make several copies of a document. Laboriously Chinese assistants would each prepare a single handwritten copy. There wasn't even any carbon paper. The [American] officials had no idea what to expect from their Chinese counterparts. Points they thought would be tough turned out to be extremely easy, and those they considered trivial produced astonishing reactions from the Chinese. . . . We could never tell where the obstacles were going to be. You could roll up your sleeves and plan for a long haul and then the problems would evaporate. Then, just when you believed you would wrap things up in a day, something would come up and you'd be there for another month.[2]

This type of situation has not totally disappeared, at least as far as the human dimension is concerned. A scholar who conducted cross-cultural training in China in the late 1980s wrote that his students "did not want to learn what was politically, culturally or practically unacceptable in China,"[3] but he also noted that the process of adopting management knowledge and skills was facilitated by the increasing number of managers taking business and management courses inside and outside China, the interaction of Chinese managers with their Western partners in joint ventures, and the settlement of an increasing number of Western-educated overseas Chinese in China as managers, experts, and entrepreneurs. Thanks to thirty-eight years of the "Open Door" economic policy, countless Chinese delegations traveling overseas, and an amazing capacity to learn and adapt,[4] the professionalization of Chinese business elites is clearly under way, as is the increasing educational achievement of managers, whether they are trained in Chinese universities or abroad.

Today the high degree of knowledge is striking. Sources of information have proliferated over the past decade (notably in the form of round-the-clock television, online newspapers, and especially social media), and Chinese business circles generally are well informed about the world's economic and geopolitical situation. Some Chinese enterprises, however, benefit from privileged access to government reports on various economic sectors; others are in direct contact with specialized think tanks, or even with university research centers. Thus the Shanghai University of International Business and Economics, though far from the best known of the universities in Shanghai, benefits from maintaining a special research center on relations with Europe. Its hospitable director, Zhang Yong-an, recounted in conversation that he regularly met with firms from neighboring provinces (Zhejiang, Jiangsu) to inform them of changes in European business practices as well as in legislation. "At least two types of firms want to go to Europe: the state-owned enterprises, and the small and medium-sized businesses that have the capital and want to explore the European market in order to develop," he states.[5]

To the second point, that of education: anyone who has had business discussions in China in recent years has no illusion about the capacity of the Chinese to conduct negotiations. Traditional values do, however, remain vibrant and include the use of parallel networks (political, provincial, student, familial, friendship-based), which can be disturbing to non-Chinese business partners; extending hospitality, which necessarily includes hosting banquets, presenting gifts, and exhibiting other marks of courtesy; and showing respect for the family and for the need to "save face," or give someone a way to preserve personal honor (*mianzi*, 面子) with his or her interlocutors, especially when they are the decisionmakers. Zhang Yong-an himself recognized the great difficulty of acculturation for these Chinese companies.

The differences are slowly eroding, however. Little by little, Chinese entrepreneurs are using accountants, lawyers, auditing services, bankers, and other professional services. This is particularly true of groups that have international ambitions, those that interest us here. Even if business negotiations remain close-fought, the Chinese contenders are "Westernized" when it comes to international transactions. (It should also be noted that the Chinese relation to time is not the same as among Westerners. Because of the many reports that have to be made to their hierarchical superiors, Chinese businesspeople sometimes give the impression of remaining silent for weeks at a time, if not months. Frequently it is because they do not have the answer.) Another newly apparent characteristic is an excess of self-confidence: "There is sometimes a feeling of being exceptional, and the Chinese often think they know better than others," remarked a former business school dean.[6] Nurtured by ambitious young Chinese expatriates who dream of doing battle and getting noticed by the head office, a conspiratorial ambiance often reigns within the offices of subsidiaries of Chinese enterprises in Europe, which by no means fosters a spirit of collaboration between Chinese managers and local recruits.

Protagonists all recount almost the same story: the first Sino-European transactions were characterized above all by a thousand snags capable of making the negotiation fail at any moment. The list of these obstacles is long: a negotiation that lasted much longer than the standard length in the profession; ignorance of Western business norms and customs on the part of the Chinese participants; constant personnel changes on the teams in place; the drafting of changes, ranging from inserting due diligence clauses to the writing of the final agreements; "resolved" clauses that were regularly put back on the table; unreliable valuations; and financing that was now in place, now lost.

The diversity of cultures and languages in Europe may disarm Chinese entrepreneurs. Poorly understood by some investors, European law is often perceived as overly favorable to the employee: workers' demonstrations, unions, and the perception of an "anti-Chinese" attitude all work to the disadvantage of Western Europe in negotiating with China. A Chinese lawyer who has settled in Europe cites as obstacles to investors the authorizations required for overtime work or work outside an employee's grade-level duties, the tax system, and the role of trade unions.[7] However, this is less true in Eastern Europe, as explained by Viktor Azmanov, chairman of the Bulgarian-Chinese Chamber of Commerce and Industry: "The Chinese have decided to invest in Romania and Bulgaria because they think there are many opportunities here, and we will welcome them with open arms."[8] Is the "new Europe" so dear to the former U.S. secretary of defense Donald Rumsfeld also what the Chinese prefer? Judging from the increasing Chinese presence in many Eastern and Central European cities, it seems to be the case. As already mentioned, China has created a "16 + 1" group of countries that allows the leaders of these Eastern and Central European countries to interact frequently on economic issues with the Chinese leadership.

Encounters between decision-makers and businessmen from China and Western Europe are also increasing, such as the biennial summit "China Meets Europe," held in Hamburg, and the China-Europa Convention, held in the Normandy town of Le Havre every other year (in alternating years it is held in China), not to mention the many ad hoc meetings orchestrated by chambers of commerce in Europe, as well as those convened by the China Council for the Promotion of International Trade (CCPIT), the state body charged with promoting commercial relations between China and the rest of the world.

Nevertheless, many intended Chinese investments remain un-successful for reasons that are often cultural. "Chinese enterprises do not want to admit that they must produce in Europe if they want to be accepted in the long term," stressed a Chinese academic, who deplored the "absence of vision" among his compatriots. Different notions of timeliness are indeed among the principal challenges: while the West wants results right away (or by a fixed date), the Chinese work over the long term, with economies of energy. The contrast is that between a sprinter and a marathon runner.

THE DRAW OF THE INTERNATIONAL SPHERE

The reasons for China's interest in developing international business activities are several, and have been examined minutely by Western scholars. A remarkable world survey, coordinated by France's Committee of Foreign Trade Advisers and published as *La Chine hors les murs* (China outside the walls),[9] identifies four main objectives the Chinese hope to achieve though internationalizing their firms:

1. Developing the geographic, logistic, and regulatory rapprochement between markets that is necessary to distribute and sell existing and future products; the primary objective is achieving greater sales volume. This is a requirement for any economic actor; Chinese enterprises do not differ.

2. Gaining secure access to the agricultural, mineral, and energy resources necessary for the development (or simply the survival) of businesses.

3. For the largest companies, acquiring (or growing from) a dominant position at the regional or global scale, going upmarket, and achieving vertical or horizontal and integration of connected activities. This line of reasoning is the most prominent one advanced

by multinational corporations that undertake implantation abroad.

4. The optimal development of production processes that take advantage of promising labor pools (this is evidently among entrepreneurs' intentions, if less remarked on). This reason perhaps belongs more to short-term tactics than to long-term strategy.

More generally, the acquisition of manufacturing processes, including patents and anything concerning research and innovation, is salient to pursuing internationalization, as is the acquisition of brands.

On the matter of brands, it may be asked why Chinese brands have so much trouble breaking into the marketplace. Until the start of the twenty-first century, China concentrated on developing an economy that was very much like that of an emerging country and oriented toward subcontracting and export. Today, when the orders fall off, Chinese enterprises must search for new ways to grow. Established brands provide a basis on which to do so.

The Chinese are fascinated by major Western brands that have attained a truly worldwide reputation such that they are instantly recognizable in any airport—especially by Chinese travelers, who are among their biggest consumers. Thus many Chinese multinationals, among them the Industrial and Commercial Bank of China and the Bank of China, the credit card firm Unionpay, the telecommunications group Huawei, the consumer electronics and home appliances brand Haier, and the computer manufacturer Lenovo, have decided to advertise in Europe, particularly within and near airports. Similarly, taking a major shareholder position in or control of a firm with the goal of developing a foreign brand in China is a reason for Chinese entrepreneurs to invest, as attested by the cases of Geely, which acquired the Swedish car maker Volvo, and the two machine tool manufacturers Zoomlion and Sany, which took control of their Italian and German competitors, respectively. Now these brands are developing on the Chinese market, rich with its billion consumers and insatiable curiosity.

This rapprochement of interests, however, poses a number of difficulties, principally because of very different management methods.

DIFFICULTIES FACED BY MERGED MULTINATIONAL CORPORATIONS OWING TO CULTURAL DIFFERENCES

It is very challenging for a Chinese group to integrate a foreign entity it has acquired, especially the senior personnel. The absence of cultural ties with Chinese decision-makers is one of the principal reasons. A few examples suffice.

The employees of the hundred-year-old company called Plysorol (founded in Lisieux, Normandy, in 1907), one of the European leaders in the fabrication of plywood, do not have good memories of the years 2009–11. After a first, voluntary liquidation, a Chinese entrepreneur by the name of Zhang Guohua took control—after a favorable decision by the commerce tribunal of Lisieux—of three sites, in Magenta, Lisieux, and Fontenay-le-Comte. With much fanfare, Zhang Guohua began conducting the operation through one of his companies, Honest Timber, a private logging concern located in Gabon, as well as through Shandong Longsheng Import and Export Company, in the province of Shandong. Buying a Normandy-based company through the Gabon subsidiary of a Chinese group is not an everyday occurrence. In his first director's letter, in 2009, Zhang declared he wanted to keep the 470 jobs in Plysorol (then in bankruptcy) and to invest €15 million. In fact, however, he really wanted to exploit 550,000 hectares (135,908 acres) of rare wood in Gabon, and he tried to transfer the production of it to China without passing through Normandy, which plunged Plysorol into new difficulties, this time about suppliers.

Evidently Zhang Guohua, dubbed "the African," was not at all interested in his French acquisition, since he committed blunder after blunder, refusing to have a dialogue with the personnel delegates, even refusing to have telephone conversations with the local officials in Normandy. Nor did China help things by organizing a press conference in the Paris offices of the China Council for the Promotion of International Trade (CCPIT), in the La Défense business district. A number of Chinese press correspondents were present, but not a single French one. After this meeting between the Chinese directors of Plysorol and the Chinese media, a mini-campaign followed in the Chinese media denouncing the lack of French flexibility and the so-called administrative annoyances that had accumulated for the new shareholders of Plysorol. In the end, Zhang Guohua had to pack his bags. Plysorol was forced to declare bankruptcy in the courts, and its fate became the subject of arbitration. Despite Zhang's promises, many jobs were abolished. Thus the investor did not leave a very good image in the region of Lisieux, particularly since he never tried to interact with his employees or even to understand them.[10]

In another example, in Spain, where the HNA Group (parent of the Hainan airline company) bought up 20 percent of the hotel chain NH Hoteles, the European administrators, whom the buyers judged unreliable, were asked to step aside. In fact, all the Chinese companies that have set up a subsidiary on the European continent have used Chinese administrators, often based at the company's headquarters in China, rather than Europeans.

Such was the case with the telecommunications giant Huawei, present in Europe for ten years, which sought strenuously to send the message that it had become a "European in Europe" multinational corporation. Each year it announced hundreds of new jobs in research that usually never came about. Each of its European subsidiaries spent from €1 million to €5 million per year to try to restore its image, despite the extreme distrust (or worse) of the governments concerned. Despite all efforts, the founder of Huawei,

Ren Zhengfei, did not succeed in meeting France's President Hollande during a trip to France in 2013. Moreover, in 2014 Huawei France signed a sponsorship contract with the football club Paris-Saint-Germain that will cost €1.3 million per year for five years (including a portion through tablets and smartphones that Huawei is trying to sell to a skeptical French public). The same scenario played out in the United Kingdom with the Arsenal Football club, with which Huawei announced a "global partnership" in January 2014.[11]

Huawei's European subsidiaries continue to be directed with an iron fist by Chinese representatives from headquarters, and it is only the few Western liegemen placed here and there at high cost (most serving as external consultants, despite their sonorous titles) who might sustain an illusion of equality. "The important positions are always reserved for the Chinese," explains one former department head at Huawei France, who was fired after four years of service (like many of his colleagues, he sued Huawei in a French industrial court for wrongful dismissal). On average, the European employees of Huawei remain just one year before getting themselves sent home ("exfiltrated") in one way or another. On the other hand, the list of employees in the French subsidiary appears strange: they include forty Chinese "interns" and fifty-some "roving" personnel, who are actually based in another European country, usually Germany, where the Huawei Group's European headquarters is located. In 2012, in a follow-up to the "600 to 700 employees" forecasted, the Human Resources Department announced a total of 391 salaried posts. Each employee is under a very specific salary regime, receiving a basic salary that is close to the minimum wage in Europe and a salary four or five times larger in China. This is a way of reducing social welfare payments to a minimum and of getting around Europe's social protection laws. It should also be noted that Huawei's famous and generous stock-option plan, dubbed "the Union," is in theory open to all employees—except the non-Chinese.

At the French headquarters of Huawei in Boulogne, Chinese employees live in a classic Chinese environment, whole families included, and are subject to constant pressure in their private life. Every Friday a family banquet (children included) is organized for expatriate Chinese personnel. The Chinese New Year celebration, often organized jointly with other Chinese companies, is the high point of the year. For a long time the subsidiary benefited from a canteen that was so Chinese it surprised new French arrivals. There is no doubt that this is a total Chinese environment. It is not unpleasant, but it unsettles the European employees, who are not used to the customs of the former Middle Kingdom.

Three years after they arrive in a European subsidiary, the great majority of Chinese employees of state-owned or semiprivate multinational corporations are usually sent home and must regain their "passport for abroad," usually by being promoted once they have achieved their individual objectives, which are set at the start of the mission.

At ZTE, the state-owned telecommunications firm, European employees recognize the weaknesses of their organization. During a meeting with one of the members of the management board of ZTE in Shenzhen, the authors had the unpleasant surprise of confronting a noticeable lack of interest, even annoyance, on the part of our hosts regarding the topic of the meeting, although the subject had been thoroughly prepared and the groundwork laid well in advance. Between what we had prepared in order to satisfy the demands of the European teams of ZTE and the reality, there stretched such a gulf that we had to wonder about the utility of such a meeting. Had the message been transmitted up the hierarchy? Perhaps not.

For its part, Huawei appears more open to international norms for managing diversity in the workplace, but its directors admit to not having found a way to integrate non-Chinese personnel. "We have not realized a major acquisition in Europe since we do not have the required capacity for integration," explained Guo Ping, deputy CEO of Huawei, in conversation. "Making an acquisition is easy, but integrating a posteriori is another thing."[12] This benign remark may have reassured Alcatel, Nokia, and Ericsson, but over the past ten years they nonetheless have seen their share of the European market melt like snowmen in the sun. Moreover, Huawei forgets to mention that it was ultimately not able to buy the British telecommunications company Marconi because of its closeness to the Chinese government and the People's Liberation Army.

There has been a change of decor at Lenovo, where the intercultural is practiced at the highest level. The executive committee includes four mainland Chinese, a Chinese person from Hong Kong, a Dutch national, an American, an Italian, and a Canadian. The Russian subsidiary is directed by a Russian, India by an Indian, and Europe by a French national. "They operated very intelligently by studying the way IBM did things," stressed Gianfranco Lanci at the European headquarters of Lenovo, in Milan.[13] In the United Kingdom, the managing director of Lenovo is also a French, ex-IBM person. However, the values and culture of Lenovo International are not necessarily those of Lenovo in China. In any case, "it is not nationality that counts, it is competence. We do not follow the model of others. Before 2005 [the year in which Lenovo acquired the personal computer division of IBM], we knew only the Chinese market; we had to learn other markets, all of them complex," explained Gina Qiao,[14] group director of human resources, who is also one of the four Chinese members of Lenovo's executive committee and the author of a recent book on intercultural relations in the multinational corporation.[15] In the European subsidiaries as elsewhere, English—or rather "Globish"—is the working language, for better or worse. Rare are the Chinese groups that invest in courses in European languages, not to mention fostering cross-cultural training. On the other hand, everything that concerns visas, work permits, and other practical formalities (real estate, driver's licenses, car accidents, registering children in schools or nurseries) is examined with a magnifying glass and managed by special teams. Thus, in the European subsidiaries of Huawei, the "administration" is a department charged exclusively with managing the lives of Chinese expatriates in Europe and of their families.

FUTURE CHALLENGES

Human resources and communication will be important things to tackle for Chinese enterprises investing in Europe. It cannot be denied that the differences are many between the structurally organized Europeans (more or less, according to country) and the pragmatic Chinese, who often are preoccupied by the desire not to lose face—which ought to be managed by a good human resources policy. Yet careers in China are rarely managed as a function of personal desiderata; even if the era of production units in which each worker is assigned a task blindly has gone, Chinese companies rarely allow their employees any choice. Managing Chinese style is affective (entailing showing respect for hierarchical superiors) and little given to strategy, but much more to pragmatism and the evaluation of individual results. In the top Chinese enterprises, it is impossible to avoid the famous Key Performance Indicator, measured at regular intervals during the year. Individualism is a quasi-religion, and each employee is furnished with a roadmap of his or her personal route that is closely examined before bonuses are given at the end of the year. And what is there to say about the *guanxi* (关系), those parallel relations among colleagues (even between a superior and an underling who come from the same province or attended the same university), which add an insurmountable complexity for the non-Chinese? "Chinese entrepreneurs must understand that money cannot do everything," explains Margaret Hong Chen, founder of the China Club in Spain, who has been living in Madrid for two decades.[16] A former boss of the subsidiary of the Spanish telecom giant Telefónica in Beijing, she hopes for an "effort at comprehension" on the part of her compatriots, pointing out that if that effort is not made, failure is predictable. It is clear that the "Chinese arrogance" that was stigmatized in a 2011 book by the late Erik Izraelewicz, former editor in chief of the French daily newspaper *Le Monde*, has not totally disappeared.

Many European employees of Chinese companies have learned at their own expense about the complexity of working together. "You feel ostracized and systematically sidelined by Chinese expatriates whose stint through a European subsidiary is a simple stage in their career," recounts a French manager who spent three years in a Chinese multinational corporation.[17] The real problem is about functioning at two speeds: on one side are employees recruited locally according to work practices in the host country, and on the other side are those who come from a head office that pays their salary and provides complementary benefits (salary savings plans, bonuses, stock options). Often members of the union, they are sent on a mission to foreign lands, but have little elbow room. Their silence (and their remuneration) usually depends on their respect for hierarchical structures. "In his professional relations, the French employee possesses a culture of effectiveness; he or she responds to colleagues and those colleagues respond to him or her. The Chinese employee moves after a prior entry into relationship. The initial distance can last a very long time before obtaining the least information," stresses the former manager of a Chinese firm.[18] Chinese corporate leaders have another way to put it. "Even when business is good, intercultural communication is essential; the two cultures can dialogue very well if they respect each other," said Guo Guangchang, founder and chairman of the major private investment company Fosun.[19] Like his counterpart Jack Ma, founder and executive chairman of Alibaba Group, Guo speaks English—which is rare. Both are truly international individuals, which doesn't mean they do not follow certain Chinese customs. For example, Fosun corporate culture includes the practice of martial arts, tai chi in particular.

The second challenge, but not less in importance, is communication. China as a country does not enjoy a good image in Europe: despite significant efforts by Beijing for two years through cultural diplomacy and with respect to the media (the press attachés at embassies have become more professional over the years), it will take time before China inspires confidence in *Homo europaeus*. As noted earlier, Chinese firms are little known to the general European public, and apart from Lenovo and Tsingtao beer, their brands rarely enjoy a good reputation. The lack of recognition does not apply in professional business circles, which know their Chinese competitors well, but how can business entities conquer a market when they cannot manage to get noticed by the media? It is true that advertising, at least advertising in foreign markets, was not a Chinese tradition until 2013 or 2014, and it is not rare for a Chinese product to be launched domestically without a marketing campaign or even a market study. This might surprise European managers who are graduates of business or engineering schools. Chinese firms function on instinct; they limit "superfluous" costs (audits, market surveys, public relations and communication tools), but they also learn quickly and are capable of reacting rapidly and learning lessons from their failures—a positive quality in relation to many others elsewhere.

Among the ten leading Chinese brands, we are starting to see the emergence of global communication, including advertising and the sponsoring of sporting events (football, tennis), but this is a long and laborious process. In addition, the idea of corporate social responsibility, which is gaining traction among Western firms, is not understood the same way in China. During an internal meeting with Chinese "international" cadres in the southern city of Guangzhou, European attendees were stunned to hear that "giving work to people is already practicing corporate social responsibility." Another pearl was that constructing infrastructure networks in Africa was helping Africa enter the modern age. The Europeans present at the meeting, though seasoned in dealing with Chinese counterparts, could not get over this statement.

SIX

CHINA IN 2016

BETWEEN BUSINESS AND POLITICS

Thirty-five years after the official end of Maoism and twenty years after the advent of "market socialism," China delights in a unique model that combines a single-party political system, renovated state enterprises, and private groups, which are increasingly oriented toward the international arena.

An example of the model and how its linkages work comes from Company X, located not far from Beijing International Airport and specializing in trade. The boss, a Chinese Communist Party (CCP) member, is close to a former prime minister, who "paved the way" for him (that is, offered him the support necessary to develop his business). To launch a new product, he relies on his network of contacts in party and government spheres. To get his products onto the Chinese market, he knows the higher-ups in customs and in the police department in the southern cities of Shenzhen and Zhuhai, which helps him a lot. And for a real nudge in the right direction, he plans to get one of the four major Chinese banks help him realize an

115

important investment in southern Europe. This kind of phenomenon, which has elements reminiscent of corruption, is nothing new in China, but the official advent of "market socialism"—the play of market forces within the confines of state control—in 1992 opened up a new horizon in relations between private entrepreneurs and the central organizations, the CCP and the country's administration.

"Chinese authorities play a key role in promoting the equity and efficiency of the socialist market economy," explains Harry Liu, a professor at the Shanghai-based China Executive Leadership Academy Pudong (CELAP), one of the top party schools. In fact, the relationship between the party and state-owned enterprises (SOEs) is intrinsic and institutional. For these companies, it is clear that party entities make most of the important, long-term decisions. An example of such state influence on an ostensibly market-sensitive corporation comes from Suntech Power, one of the principal world producers of solar energy under the leadership of founder and former CEO Shi Zhengrong. In the year 2000, after relocating to Australia for graduate studies, Shi was lured by CCP officials back to the city of Wuxi, near Shanghai, where he grew up, to start and run a solar energy company with government financing. In the following decade, things went very smoothly for Shi. At its peak, Suntech was valued on the New York Stock Exchange at $16 billion. By 2009, Suntech had become the world's largest solar-panel maker, with an annual capacity of 1,000 megawatts. Several years later, in 2013, Suntech's board forced Shi to resign as executive chairman, after the company's main operating unit, Wuxi Suntech, had accumulated a debt of $2.2 billion and filed for bankruptcy protection. "In addition to a dramatic fall of the global solar industry, Suntech's demise was also intimately linked to the Chinese government's explicit determination to make solar and other renewable energy technologies a 'strategic' industry," an investigative report stated.[1] "Sun king" Shi himself confessed during a Shanghai press conference in May 2013: "I have let you guys down." When it comes to discussing the subject outside China, the party's influence is rarely acknowledged. "In

China, the relation between business and politics is a complex subject that appears in doctoral dissertations and is better to learn on your own without a textbook," joked Wang Jianlin, chairman of the real estate developer Dalian Wanda Group (and one of China's richest men), in an interview in *Le Monde*. Traveling through Europe in 2013, he offered this advice: "Stick to your own affairs and maintain the best possible relations with the local authorities."[2]

The linkage between Chinese government and business firms is not a new phenomenon but dates back at least to the Shang dynasty, when the emperor encouraged private enterprise. Later on, in the nineteenth century (Qing dynasty), the warlords adopted bad habits, using their power to develop certain trades, especially in textiles. The same was true of the Republic of China from 1911 to 1949, when the corruption of the Kuomintang left nothing to envy in its predecessors. The arrival in power of the CCP in 1949 sealed the return of the centralized economy: private enterprises gradually disappeared in the 1960s, and the retrenchment continued to the end of the 1980s. Firms such as HSBC, Wah Kung Shipping, Peninsula Knitters, and Li & Fung chose to establish themselves in Hong Kong, then a British colony and fully open to unbridled capitalism. Others took the route to Taiwan, Singapore, the United States, or the United Kingdom. A few rare entrepreneurs, such as the Shanghainese tycoon Rong Yiren, founder of CITIC (China International Trust and Investment Corp.), chose to remain in China and to work with the Communist regime. Rong was thanked by the regime and became vice president of the People's Republic of China from 1993 to 1998.

In December 1978, the Third Plenary of the First Central Committee sealed the return to power of Deng Xiaoping and inaugurated an era of unprecedented reform. After a turbulent period in this huge country, still scarred by the Cultural Revolution (1966–76), the private enterprises created in the 1980s and 1990s finally took off: between 1978 and 2013, the number of businesses in China increased from 140,000 to 31 million in 1999, then to 40 million in 2013.[3] From the beginning of the 1980s, entrepreneurship was encouraged (see the box for a list of the top ten private companies in 2013), and the model here is Legend, an electronics company created in 1984, thanks to an investment of about €20,000 by the Chinese Academy of Sciences. That small company would eventually become Lenovo and would buy the personal computer division of IBM in 2005. Although technically private, it became tied to the state and the party by receiving money from the state. Today it is the world's number one company in personal computers. In 1992, Deng's "southern tour" (in Chinese, *nanxun*) confirmed an almost irreversible movement when he pronounced the word "openness" (*kai fang*, 开放) in Shenzhen, southern China.

THE TEN TOP CHINESE PRIVATE GROUPS IN 2014
Sales figures in 2013 yuan

1. Suning Appliance Group (¥279.8 billion)—major distribution
2. Legend Holdings (¥244 billion)—information technology
3. Shandong Weiqiao Pioneering Group (¥241.5 billion)—textiles
4. Huawei Technologies (¥239 billion)—telecommunications
5. Amer International Group (¥233.8 billion)—metallurgy
6. Shagang Group (¥228 billion)—metallurgy
7. China Energy Company (¥209.9 billion)—energy
8. Wanda Group (¥186.6 billion)—real estate and hotels
9. Geely Holding Group (¥154.8 billion)—automobile
10. China Vanke (¥135.4 billion)—real estate

SOURCE: *All-China Federation of Industry and Commerce, "Top Ten Private Companies in China,"* China Daily, August 20, 2014 (http://www.china.org.cn/business/2014-08/20/content_33290116.htm).

PRIVATE ENTERPRISE AND THE COMMUNIST PARTY

The proliferation of private enterprises does not diminish the role of the CCP. Today, individual applications to the party are legion, whether from directors of private companies or from executives of SOEs, two quite distinct groups that manage the two sides of the Chinese economy. In 2014, 65 percent of Chinese businesses were private, but they had to maintain important links with the party, which since 1949 has provided the framework of government organization, in Beijing and in the entire country. For private entities, it was not necessarily a matter of belonging officially to the CCP but rather of a collaboration between leaders who were animated by a common interest. As detailed in the preceding chapters, having relationships in high places is essential to obtaining bank loans or authorizations for mergers and acquisitions. In reality, political and governmental relationships are indispensable for any Chinese private entrepreneur. At a recent meeting with the head of a major private group in Shanghai, attendees were surprised to be led out through a small door: at the building's main entrance a red carpet had been rolled out to welcome the local party secretary for a "routine" visit. In 2015, top private entrepreneurs were often asked to "collaborate" on matters related to corruption scandals.

With regard to SOEs, the situation is still more robust, since the senior managers are required to be part of the party hierarchy; sometimes they only pass through an SOE as a step in their career, which is managed by the organization department of the CCP.[4] Each SOE has a parallel organization, the party section, directed by a person who is often hierarchically superior to the president of the enterprise—or at least his equal. That is the reason why in China, the number two often counts for as much as the number one, especially in important negotiations, and it is not always easy to distinguish them.

In the triangle formed by the business world, the party, and the government administration, an opacity mixed with tacit consent is the prevailing tenor. Whether regarding financing or the authorization to export, the advantages linked to this phenomenon are significant and characterized by certain benefits. This model of "mutualized gains" is one of the keys to Chinese business.

CORRUPTION SPREADING AT ALL LEVELS

The plenary session of the two houses of the Chinese parliament, the Chinese People's Political Consultative Conference (CPPCC) and the National People's Congress (NPC), is held each year in March. In 2014 the NPC included a hundred members who were also listed in the *Hurun Report*, which each year publishes an inventory of Chinese millionaires and billionaires. Thus Liu Yonghao, a former teacher of mathematics and founder of the agribusiness giant New Hope Group, at age sixty-six, rich with his 600 million renminbi, was elevated in 2014 to the post of vice-chairman of the Committee for Economic Affairs of the CCP and vice-president of the All-China Federation of Industry and Commerce.[5] Wang Jianlin, of Dalian Wanda, is a deputy in the NPC, as is Zong Qinghou, founder of the beverage group Wahaha.

It was easy for Fu Ying, the spokesperson of the 2014 NPC and today the chair of its Foreign Affairs Committee, to announce "zero tolerance for corruption." The links between politics and business are well known and include such outrageous manifestations as buying the votes of delegates at the provincial level, as well as the many scandals in recent years that have highlighted the ties between the political class and the business class. The relationship is particularly clear in certain provinces, where economic and political circles, and sometimes also the security services, work hand-in-hand. Several provincial party hierarchs were dismissed from their positions as a result of anticorruption investigations, including the former mayor of Nanjing, Ji Jianye, who in April 2015 received a jail sentence of fifteen years for corruption; leaders of SOEs, such as Xu Long, director general of a subsidiary of China Mobile; and union bosses, such as Chen Anzhong. In the fall of 2015, after a midyear stock-market crash exposed weaknesses in China's financial system, the authorities detained several key bankers and fund managers, including Mao Xiaofeng, president of China Minsheng Bank; Yim Fung, chairman of Guotai Junan International; and Zhang Yun, president of the Agricultural Bank of China, to name just a few.[6]

THE RED ARISTOCRACY

Unlike his two predecessors, Jiang Zemin and Hu Jintao, China's current president and general secretary of the CCP Xi Jinping came from a line of revolutionary leaders: his father, Xi Zhongxun, was (before being fired from his post as vice premier in 1962, during the Cultural Revolution) one of the companions of Mao Zedong in the later stages of the Long March (Xi's path thus was close to Deng Xiaoping's). Because he knew the system better than anybody, Xi Jinping, who is considered the most powerful Chinese leader since Deng Xiaoping, on becoming president and party chief in November 2012 launched an important anticorruption campaign, punishing more than 180,000 officials in government, SOEs, the media, the People's Liberation Army (PLA), and even the private sector.

The links between leaders, the families of leaders, and the economic world—including internationally—are infinite. Investigative reports published by the news agency Bloomberg and the *New York Times* on the personal and family fortunes of Xi Jinping himself and of Wen Jiabao, prime minister from 2002 to 2012, threw a spanner into the works by revealing what many Chinese already knew. "Many relatives of Wen Jiabao, including his son, daughter, younger brother and brother-in-law, have become extraordinarily wealthy during his leadership," the *New York Times* reported in a remarkable investigation, which estimated the total amount of the family fortune at $2.7 billion.[7] Thus in 2004, the State Council or cabinet (then presided over by Premier Wen Jiabao) had exempted Ping An Insurance Company from certain restrictions, which enabled the company's stock to rise on the stock exchange by $1.8 billion. The *New York Times* indicated that the Wen family was a leading investor and thus a beneficiary. According to the newspaper, Fullmark Consultants, a company directed by the daughter of Wen Jiabao, Lily Chang (whose real name is Wen Ruchun), had received $1.8 million from the American bank J.P. Morgan. In 2015 the U.S. Securities and Exchange Commission began conducting a vast investigation into this bank, which might have profited from traffic in influence.[8]

Xi Jinping, the man who imposed austerity on his peers (in 2004 he told his comrades that they should keep an eye on their spouses, their children, and their friends, so that friends and family did not use their power to enrich themselves), did not succeed in preventing his larger family from doing deals before he became party leader: in 2012, Bloomberg estimated the fortune of his "close relations" at $376 million, including in the family's holdings a company trading in minerals, another in telephones, and at least seven real estate properties in Hong Kong, for a total amount of $55.6 million.[9]

When Bloomberg discussed several members of the extended Xi family (including the president's sister and brother-in-law and their daughter), the report stated it was "not able to prove that Xi enriched himself personally." This was not the case with the fired party secretary of Chongqing and another famous "prince," Bo Xilai, son of a Long March companion of Mao's, today in prison after a somber affair of murder, whose fortune was estimated at $136 million. The son of Bo Xilai, Bo Guagua, remains in exile in the United States and often travels to London (and is surely not in need). China is a country where the gap between rich and poor is rocketing. And amid the throes of a national anticorruption campaign, revelations by the foreign press have caused some trouble at the top. The most spectacular case is no doubt that of Zhou Yongkang.[10] In March 2014, authorities confiscated 90 billion yuan ($14.5 billion) belonging to the family and to 300 persons who were more or less close to this former member of the Standing Committee of the Politburo and secretary of the Central Political and Legal Affairs Commission, responsible for security—and close to Bo Xilai, about whose merits he had boasted before the fall of the Chongqing party boss. Among other people close to Zhou who were arrested were Jiang Jiemin, former president of the two energy giants Petro-China and China National Petroleum Corporation, both heavily invested in Africa, Asia, Australia, and North America; the former vice-minister of security, Li Dongsheng; and a former vice-governor of Hainan province, Ji Wenlin.

In a remarkable report that was banned in China, the International Consortium of Investigative Journalists (ICIJ) in January 2014 revealed the scope of the network of the so-called "princelings," including, notably, five current or former members of the Standing Committee of the Politburo.[11] The report detailed the offshore activities of the families of senior leaders, in particular in the British Virgin Islands and the Cook Islands in the Caribbean. Those featured were Fu Liang, son of Peng Zhen (former mayor of Beijing); Liu Chunhang, a staff member of the Chinese banking regulator and the son-in-law of Wen Jiabao; Wen Yunsong, a businessman and the son of Wen Jiabao; Deng Jiagui, the brother-in-law of Xi Jinping and a real estate investor; and Li Xiaolin, the daughter of the former prime minister Li Peng. The list is long (it gives 21,000 addresses in China and Hong Kong) and covers sectors as varied as petroleum, green energy, the weapons industry, and mining and mineral concerns.

Of course, many Western financial institutions had acted as intermediaries, such as PricewaterhouseCoopers, UBS, and Credit Suisse. This should not come as a surprise: Jiang Mianheng, the son of former president Jiang Zemin, worked for Goldman Sachs; Lily Chang once worked for Lehman Brothers; the daughter of Chen Yun (himself the heir of the economist Chen Yuan and president of the China Development Bank) worked for Morgan Stanley; and the daughter of Vice-Premier Wang Yang had worked for Deutsche Bank. To be sure, these "princes" and "princesses" have generally studied at the best American or European universities, but the financial institutions also know how to choose their collaborators for their high-level connections at the heart of China's establishment.

The ICIJ estimates that a staggering $1,000 billion to $4,000 billion in capital has left China over fifteen years: "China's rapid economic growth leads to tensions inside the country, since the results of growth are not equitably divided. The hundred richest persons possess 300 billion dollars, whereas 300 million Chinese live on less than two dollars a day," the ICIJ report explained. It appears that the Chinese tax regime—and more generally stricter economic laws—have greatly encouraged the wealthy Chinese to invest their money outside the country, sometimes to better repatriate it (thanks to subtle offshore banking arrangements).

Higher-ups in the PLA were not spared the witch hunt under Xi: General Guo Boxiong, the PLA highest-ranking military officer between 2002 and 2012, was accused of "using his influence to seek promotion for others and accepting bribes."[12] General Xu Caihou, another former vice-chairman of the party's Central Military Commission, was also arrested for corruption. He was suspected of having earned 35 million yuan in bribes from another former officer, Gu Junshan, ex-number two in the PLA's General Logistics Department.[13] The constant reshuffling of personnel within military regions does not matter: since the start of economic openness in the 1980s, a web of connections has been woven between party officials, army officers, and the leadership of provincial business circles.

Many "advantages in kind" (use of official cars, trips, banquets, various presents) given to Chinese officials are said to have been reduced by 35 percent. Some have been imprisoned for corruption or publicly blacklisted, to serve as examples. However, the whole system seems intractably noxious and resistant to transparency and equity. Among the occasional victims of these injustices are foreign companies based in China. Because of a system foreigners understand only partially, they are now seeing the doors to some markets closing.

WHAT ABOUT INSTITUTIONAL
RELATIONS IN EUROPE?

Chinese enterprises that invest in Europe seem to have understood that the institutional environment on the continent requires investing on the relational level as well, which they interpret as currying favor with government officials at all levels. Across Europe, governments and administrations, especially in the European Commission, have become accustomed to receiving Chinese representatives who come to "explore opportunities" and to present their businesses—sometimes without a great deal of finesse—to a ministerial adviser or a European civil servant. Among the subjects frequently raised are visa matters, access to markets, and requests to meet European ministers or commissioners, always at a higher level. Usually these requests are combined with promises of investment that are rendered in more or less precise terms—music to the ears of European officials, who have difficulty finding new employers in their country or in their constituency.

Huawei, since it makes telecommunication infrastructure, has long excelled in this domain. Each year the company endeavors to put European countries in competition with each other, causing various investment agencies to work relentlessly, from London to Paris by way of Milan and Stockholm. The flamboyant building that houses Huawei in Reading, England, and the company's European demonstration center in Amsterdam—250 square meters of windows, inaugurated with pomp by the city's mayor—reflect this strategy. In 2014, French prime minister Manuel Valls welcomed the founder of this company, Ren Zhengfei, who promised an "investment plan of €15 billion over five years and 650 new jobs."[14] But this kind of announcement had already been issued in 2009 with the opening of a so-called research center that never saw the light of day. Moreover, a center at Lannion, in Brittany, that was supposed to serve Orange (ex-France Télécom) was discreetly closed by Huawei.

The promises are dangled before an audience of European politicians. André Santini is mayor of Issy-les-Moulineaux in the Paris region, a city that welcomed several Chinese firms and has made a specialty of this. The former French prime minister Jean-Pierre Raffarin, who travels to China frequently, does not hesitate to welcome many Chinese delegations to the Senate and to his Poitiers constituency. Some representatives of Chinese firms even ask for meetings with heads of state and government, which they occasionally obtain, and these meetings then become trophies for the Chinese directors of the European subsidiaries of these groups. Senior political contacts are highly valued in corporate China, as they are in the Chinese system overall. Most of the time, they provide access to business.

As in the United States, certain Chinese companies arm themselves with local lobbyists, and the outstanding leader in all categories is Huawei, which has several spokesmen or local leaders of public affairs in each European country, as well as specialized teams for different domains: press relations, institutional relations, relations with NGOs, corporate social responsibility, digital affairs, publicity events, and so on. These are all sectors justified by the telecom giant's aspiration to secure a global footprint, as IBM did in the 1980s. But are the results convincing? Nothing is less sure. Certainly the French establishment remains circumspect about this group, particularly since the report written by the centrist senator Jean-Marie Bockel, former secretary of state for defense, in 2012,[15] or the many warning reports published by ANSSI,[16] the French National Agency for the Security of Information Systems, which in 2013 and 2014 required three French operators, including Orange, to dismantle Huawei and ZTE (its top Chinese competitor) equipment in French overseas territories for reasons of security. At a time when many countries are rightly worried about cybersecurity, the route has become sinuous for Chinese technological groups, which are suspected of having ties to the Chinese security services, despite their denials and their grand strategies for investment, which often take a long time to realize.

In China, politics always dominates the economy when it comes to strategic sectors (energy, defense, communications, transport): a Chinese group will always try to establish close relations with the Chinese embassy in each European country and will try to help national authorities (including financially) when it comes to setting up some communication activity or a cultural event. This patronage is not surprising, but it does illustrate the gap between what Europeans think of as "Westernized" China and the reality of a Chinese system in which politics always comes back like a shot.

SEVEN

CHINA'S PERFECTIBLE IMAGE

BUILDING SOFT POWER AND COMMUNICATION SKILLS

The old image of look-alike Chinese delegations visiting European factories to be better inspired by their technologies (and to profit from frequent official invitations) has changed. Now it is men and women in a hurry who come to Europe to do business. However, these entrepreneurs cannot escape their identity or their nationality when they meet European interlocutors.

By the turn of the twenty-first century, China had achieved a level of economic development that was unprecedented. Between 1979 and 2013, it enjoyed an average growth of 10 percent, and even since 2012, growth has hovered around 6.5 percent. The stock market turmoil in the summer of 2015 revealed the many weaknesses of the Chinese economy, which is also thought to be growing at a much slower pace. The second biggest world economy and the foremost trading power, China might still supplant the United States in the future. Some optimistic visions, like that of the Organization of Economic Cooperation and Development, estimate that it will be the first-ranked trading power in the world as early as 2016. Beijing has a permanent seat on the UN Security Council, holds key posts in several international organizations, and maintains a major diplomatic network.[1] But, like all emerging powers, China must also demonstrate leadership, which includes the exercise of soft power, and in general must communicate better with the rest of the world, which is the subject of this chapter.

To understand the real image of China in the world, it is helpful to examine the Pew Research Center's most recent Global Attitudes survey (Spring 2015), on the images of countries around the world.[2] According to the study, countries where China's image is the worst are in the West, even if the figures are tending to improve. In July 2014, 49 percent of Germans and 49 percent of the British considered China to be the foremost world economy (compared to 20 percent and 34 percent, respectively, that allotted first place to the United States). In 2014, 60 percent of people surveyed by Pew thought that China had replaced or would replace the United States as the top superpower (against 33 percent who thought it would never replace the United States).

Many who are asked think that China will one day become the top-ranked global power (see table 7-1). Its increasingly extensive economic presence, its growing political and military weight, and the assertion of its military and economic strength in the Asia Pacific region especially make Beijing unavoidable. The United States may have a superior military force, but it must now deal with this actor, described as "revisionist" by Harvard professor Joseph Nye,[3] implying change within an equilibrium of powers in a region until now dominated by the United States. In the future, it is unlikely America will be the only power dominating Asia militarily. It will be forced to share its power with China.

China and Japan, the prime American ally in the region, constantly fight over the Diaoyu (or Senkaku) islands in the East China Sea, and China has imposed an Air Defense Identification Zone in an application of the "new model of relations among powers" called for by President Xi Jinping. "It is logical that America be obliged to

TABLE 7-1. *Has China Replaced the United States
As a Superpower, or Will It?*

	2008 (%)	2009 (%)	2011 (%)	2013 (%)	2014 (%)	2015 (%)
Canada	—	52	—	67	—	52
United States	36	33	46	47	49	46
France	66	55	72	70	61	66
Spain	57	48	67	71	67	60
United Kingdom	55	49	65	66	62	59
Germany	61	51	61	66	60	59
Italy	—	—	—	48	48	57
Poland	38	36	47	55	46	46
Greece	—	—	—	57	55	—
Czech Republic	—	—	—	54	—	—
Russia	36	41	45	50	45	44
Ukraine	—	—	—	—	40	39
China	58	67	63	66	59	67

SOURCE: *Pew Research Center, Spring 2015 Global Attitudes survey, Q18.*

NOTES: *Results for Ukraine in 2014 may differ from previously published figures. To make the 2014 sample comparable to 2015, Luhansk, Donetsk, and Crimea were excluded from the 2014 sample. These areas were not surveyed in 2015 because of security concerns. Trends prior to 2014 are also omitted.*

reduce its weight while China increases its own. For Beijing wants to be the equal of Washington," writes Hugh White, a China scholar at the Lowy Institute in Sydney.[4] For his part, the British sinologist Kerry Brown went so far as to speak in 2012 of an inferiority complex: "In less than a generation, China went from the status of an average power to that of an actor in the international community . . . that barely counts on support." According to this expert, China does not enjoy a good image because of its unique system, characterized by elements of a capitalist market orientation that are constrained by a socialist state, and because of the fear the country inspires (table 7-2).[5]

TABLE 7-2. *China Favorability since 2007*

	2007 (%)	2008 (%)	2009 (%)	2010 (%)	2011 (%)	2012 (%)	2013 (%)	2014 (%)	2015 (%)	2007–2015 CHANGE
United States	42	39	50	49	51	40	37	35	38	−4
Canada	52	—	53	—	—	—	43	—	39	−13
Italy	27	—	—	—	—	30	28	26	40	+13
France	47	28	41	41	51	40	42	47	50	+3
Spain	39	31	40	47	55	49	48	39	41	+2
Poland	39	33	43	46	51	50	43	32	40	+1
Germany	34	26	29	30	34	29	28	28	34	0
United Kingdom	49	47	52	46	59	49	48	47	45	−4
Greece	—	—	—	—	—	56	59	49	—	—
Czech Republic	35	—	—	—	—	33	34	—	—	—
Russia	60	60	58	60	63	62	62	64	79	+19
Ukraine	—	—	—	—	—	—	—	64	58	—

SOURCE: *Pew Research Center, Spring 2015 Global Attitudes survey, Q12b.*

With regard to China's becoming a superpower, more findings by the Pew Research Center appertain: in twenty-three of thirty-nine countries sampled, the majority of respondents surveyed considered that China had replaced (or would sooner or later replace) the United States as a superpower. Even Americans appeared very split: 47 percent thought that China would supplant the United States and 47 percent thought the opposite.

According to this Pew study, the best support for China is found in Asia (Malaysia, Pakistan) and Africa, especially Kenya (78 percent), Senegal (77 percent), and Nigeria (76 percent) (table 7-3). On the other hand, only 5 percent of the Japanese respondents had a positive opinion of their Asian neighbor. European countries hesitate a great deal: 11 percent of the British respondents had a good opinion of China, as did 9 percent of the French. On the other hand, 64 percent of

TABLE 7-3. *China Favorability by Region*

	FAVORABLE (%)	UNFAVORABLE (%)
Africa	70	13
Latin America	57	30
Asia/Pacific	57	33
Middle East	52	46
European Union	41	50
United States	38	54

SOURCE: *Pew Research Center, Spring 2015 Global Attitudes survey, Q12b.*

NOTES: *Median percentages by region. China is not included in the Asia/Pacific median.*

TABLE 7-4. *Younger People in Europe Tend to Have a Higher Opinion of China*

	TOTAL (%)	18–29 YEARS (%)	30–49 YEARS (%)	50+ YEARS (%)	YOUNGEST–OLDEST GAP (PERCENTAGE POINTS)
Spain	41	56	41	37	**+19**
Poland	40	48	43	35	**+13**
France	50	56	54	46	**+10**
Italy	40	46	40	38	+8
United Kingdom	45	45	46	42	+3
Germany	34	32	30	36	−4

SOURCE: *Pew Research Center, Spring 2015 Global Attitudes survey.*

NOTE: *Significant differences in bold.*

the German respondents had a negative opinion of China, whereas this figure was only 36 percent in 2006. China today is perceived by some as a competitor, an invader, and a dangerous military power. However, younger people in Europe tended to have a higher opinion of China than older people (see table 7-4).

Opinions about China vary considerably according to world region. Fewer than 50 percent of respondents surveyed in North America and Europe had a positive opinion of China (this finding did not obtain in other world regions, such as Central and South Latin America).

CHINA'S CONFLICTED INTERNATIONAL IMAGE

In January 2014 there was no sign of joy in Carhaix, in the Brittany region of France, when the Chinese agro-food group Synutra confirmed its investment of €100 million. On the contrary, the local Member of Parliament, Richard Ferrand, expressed some worry linked both to what he called "European post-quotas" and to fear of the Chinese giant: "Even after the first stone is laid, when I talked with some of my constituents, especially the farmers, I had the feeling that they feared seeing China take control of their means of production."[6] On the other hand, there was no worry on the part of workers in milk production, who were impatiently waiting for the opening of a Synutra factory in Carhaix in 2016 and the jobs to be created.

The Chinese government became aware of the weaknesses in its international image and communication during a succession of crises in the mid-2000s, marked by its failure to be forthcoming about the severe acute respiratory syndrome (SARS) epidemic in 2005, followed by the bird flu epidemic of 2013; public criticism over contaminated Chinese products (toys, adulterated milk); and the public relations disaster surrounding the Olympic flame on its journey to the Beijing Games (2008), as well as its inadequate response to criticism over Tibet and China's poor human rights record. All these episodes (and muted responses) merely increased the world's perplexity about China. Moreover, the context was a worldwide economic crisis that seemed to feed a growing anti-Chinese sentiment in Western public opinion. Often, skeptics are split between those who see the steady increase in China's military budget or the absence of human rights in the country as proof of China's aggressiveness toward the West and those who denounce the extreme pressures of Western employment that accompany global relocations. Finally, some criticize the poor quality of Chinese products, forcing the Chinese authorities to react through publicity campaigns such as its "Made in China, made with the world" campaign, which was broadcast on *BBC World* and on CNN.

CHINESE SOFT POWER

Soft power was one of the important stakes in the policy established in November 2012 during the 18th Congress of the Chinese Communist Party (CCP). But we should look carefully at this term, "soft power," which was invented by Joseph Nye in 1990 and first appeared in print in an article in *Foreign Affairs* on the United States. In a subsequent book, *Bound to Lead: The Changing Nature of American Power* (1991),[7] Nye stressed that the United States was not the most powerful nation not only in economic and military spheres but also through its use of "soft power," which he defined as "the possibility of obtaining a result through seduction and not coercion," a power that is exercised in the domains of culture, education, and sometimes the economy. For nations that know how to use it, this power endows a real capacity to influence.

Until then limited to alliances with "brother parties" as far away as Africa and Latin America, Chinese soft power was formally born in the writings of several academics close to former Chinese president Hu Jintao: Zheng Bijian, who in 2003 launched the concept of a "peaceful rise." It was further adumbrated in the 2007 texts of Wang Jisi, at the time dean of the School of International Studies at Peking University, who advocated a "harmonious world." In a parallel move, the Chinese Ministry of Foreign Affairs created the

Department of Public Diplomacy in 2009, and even a "Chinese association of public diplomacy" in 2013, the latter designed to propagate these principles in provincial towns and cities.

Much ink has been spilled about this parallel diplomacy. Beijing is increasingly aware of its bad image and now invests significant amounts to improve it (a figure of $10 billion a year has been mentioned). Convincing Europeans of Chinese goodwill is not easy to do in the crosshairs of an economic crisis—except when it comes to promoting the attractions of a Chinese domestic market in full growth, for which the use of Mandarin is an obvious asset. The central government seems to have understood this.

THE CONFUCIUS INSTITUTES

For language education, the preeminent tool of influence is the network of Confucius Institutes, which over ten years has assumed considerable scope, with 600 establishments opened and an annual budget of $278 million in 2013. The support comes from the top: Liu Yunshan, one of the seven members of the Standing Committee of the Politburo, declared in June 2014 that the Confucius Institutes were "high-speed trains" that had appeared at a "good moment" because they promoted the Chinese Dream on the international level.[8]

Inspired by such examples as the Alliance Française, the British Council, and the Goethe-Institut, these language establishments have little to do with either philosophy or morality, although the Confucian temple of the Guozijian (National Academy), in the heart of Beijing, presented an out of-date exhibition on this proliferating network. On the other hand, the Confucius Institutes do have a lot to do with politics and with the influence of China in the world.

Brand-new Confucius Institutes have appeared almost everywhere in the world in the past five years. They emanate directly from the central government, from the very official *Hanban*, the international Council of the Chinese Language, which reports to the Min-

istry of Education and grants each of these establishments a starting budget of about $1 million and an operating budget of about
$250,000 per year. Chinese academics are offered stays abroad in
these centers to propagate the message.

Abroad, the Confucius Institutes "collaborate" with universities
and local teaching establishments by supplying them with teachers
and textbooks. The problem is that the actual language teaching
leaves something to be desired: the teachers are often sociologists,
political scientists, historians, or economists, but rarely linguists or
teachers of Chinese as a second language. Their mission seems to be
principally to proselytize in the cultural realm. Many foreign universities have seen the teaching of Chinese falter in the face of in-
struction from this new kind of "embassy," which wields a carrot
and a stick over those whom it is subsidizing. In theory, the Confucius Institutes are subject to the laws of the countries in which they
are located. But several European study centers have had to halt
their collaboration with the Confucius Institute, among them the
establishment at the heart of the University of Lyon in southern
France, which benefited from a partnership with Sun Yat-Sen University in Guangzhou.

In September 2013, the University of Lyon decided to close the
institute because of repeated interference from the Chinese administration, which was subsidizing the center without the Confucius
Institute's being embedded into the university, for deontological and
pedagogical reasons. Evidently the director sent by Beijing seemed
to contest the teaching methods at the university, meanwhile wanting Lyon students to pursue their studies in China. "Tolerated for
two years, it seems that our intellectual independence stopped being
tolerated by Beijing starting in 2012, no doubt due to a policy change
on the part of Hanban. Its lack of flexibility has hindered the possibility of a compromise," according to two former officials of the
Confucius Institute of Lyon, Gregory Lee and Florent Villard. In
the United States, the ambiance is scarcely better, for example, at the
University of Oregon, where the director of the Confucius Institute,

Bryna Goodman (who receives funding from Hanban), and her colleague, China expert Glenn May (who does not receive funding and remains independent from all points of view), are at drawn daggers on this subject.

CULTURE

More recent and more promising is the Chinese breakthrough in the domain of culture. Public and private museums are multiplying in China. After an international tender, the French architect Jean Nouvel was charged with constructing the prestigious National Art Museum of China (NAMOC) in Beijing. A hundred or so new museums open each year throughout the country, which now counts almost 4,000 of them. In March 2014, a couple of Shanghai billionaires, Wang Wei and Liu Yiqian, inaugurated their second private museum, on an abandoned airfield, to exhibit contemporary works, notably those by Fang Lijun and Zhou Chunya. The operation is said to have cost more than €30 million.

In Beijing, the Dashanzi "798" neighborhood with its hundreds of galleries has become one of the most visited places in the capital, to the point that it has acquired quasi-official status and has many imitators. Wagering on the success of the first Chinese painters to become known internationally in the 1990s (such as Yue Minjun, Zhang Xiaogang, and Zeng Fanzhi), many galleries have opened their doors in China. Meanwhile, some galleries are beginning to open in Europe, allowing Chinese influence to be relayed there, often straightforwardly, as in the first gallery of Xinhua art (from the name of the official Chinese information agency), which opened in 2013 on 400 square meters in the fashionable Faubourg Saint-Honoré, two steps from the Élysée Palace, the residence of France's president. In the great European museums, Chinese art exhibits are frequent, like the one titled *Ming: The Fifty Years That Changed China* at the British Museum (2014–15) or *The Forbidden City* at the Louvre (2011–12). For the latter, two Chinese firms, Haier and Air China, assumed the role of patrons. The excellent exhibit *Chinese Artists in Paris* at the Cernuschi Museum in 2011 was also underwritten in part by Chinese firms. Finally, the state visit of President Xi Jinping to France in March 2014 occasioned many cultural events, including the mounting of a major exhibition of Chinese contemporary artists at the Grand Palais that was entirely financed by the Chinese Ministry of Culture.

Chinese cultural centers are also the focus of a glamorous lifestyle, even if they remain more instruments of the Chinese state than sites of artistic freedom. The Chinese Cultural Center in Paris, for example, opened its doors in 2010 on the avenue de La Tour-Maubourg and has welcomed a number of artists, ranging from the film director Chen Sicheng to the sculptor Wu Wei-shan, director of the Academy of Fine Arts at the University of Nanjing, and the figurative painter Xing Jianjian. Some of these artists are celebrities in China, but their names mean little to Europeans unless they are specialists. The distances, both geographic and cultural, have something to do with it.[9]

The same is true of Chinese literature, where there are two recent Nobel Prize winners, one of them politically correct (close to power), Mo Yan, who received the prize in 2012, and the other in exile and not approved of in Beijing, Gao Xingjian, who was awarded it in 2000. Apart from them, recent successes in Chinese literature who have been published in the West include Wang Anyi, Yu Hua, Su Tong, Wang Shuo, Ma Jian, Mian Mian, Wang Xiaobo, Qiu Xiaolong, and Dai Sijie, who has adopted French nationality. With the exception of a handful of writers, Chinese novels do not reach European readers to contribute positively to Chinese soft power. The same is true of the cinema, which enjoyed a period of glory in the 1990s under such directors as Cheng Kaige, Zhang Yimou, Tian Zhuangzhuang, Lou Ye, and Jia Zhang-ke. Their successors, outside Hong Kong and Taiwan, do not seem to "break the screen," despite the proliferation of festivals of Chinese cinema. In Paris, the film club of the Chinese Cultural Center offers long and short features throughout the year; the fourth festival of Chinese cinema in France, supported by such businesses as Air China and the Bank of China, took place in 2014 in a dozen cities, including Lyon, Marseille, Cannes, Strasbourg, and Biarritz. On the program were contemporary films about Chinese society by Fei Xing, Chen Sicheng, Cao Baoping, and Fang Gangliang. Finally, a magazine called *China on the Seine* provides a panorama of all the activities at the Cultural Center; its articles include interviews with European artists who are close to China.

INTERNATIONAL EVENTS: 2008 BEIJING OLYMPICS, 2010 SHANGHAI WORLD EXPO, 2022 WINTER OLYMPICS

The Olympic Games in Beijing in 2008 were the first global event organized by China. Although the Games were a great success ("a faultless organization, friendly atmosphere, with unforgettable sports performances," opined the *Youth Daily*, boasting of the "image of a great country, entirely new"), the passage of the Olympic torch through several countries gave rise to incidents that provoked some consternation in China. Surely nobody could have imagined that the Games would provide an opportunity for the "enemies of China" (including perfectly legitimate organizations defending human rights) to attack the regime in Beijing. The demonstrations in favor of Tibet in particular disrupted the "voyage of harmony" in Paris and London, obliging the organizers of the Olympic torch relay to change the route.

In the summer of 2015, the International Olympic Committee (IOC) decided to award the 2022 Winter Olympics to Beijing. The decision was made despite environmental concerns and the facts that China has neither a tradition of hosting such a winter sports event nor adequate amounts of precipitation. Environmentalists are outraged, since most of the snow in 2022 will be man-made, with snowmaking predicted to consume more than 1 percent of the water supply of Beijing, which already suffers from drought.[10] The lack of contenders led the IOC to pick the only country that would make the Games happen.

The administration in Shanghai showed more foresight in 2010, when, over a period of six months, the Shanghai World Expo welcomed 73 million visitors and 250 participating bodies, including representatives from almost all the countries in the world and many international organizations.

Rarely has a world exposition been so used by a government for purposes of communication on the national and the international levels. Chinese families circulated happily around the sites on both sides of the Huangpu river, admiring the thematic and national pavilions, starting with the most imposing one, China's. Like London and Paris at the end of the nineteenth-century, China intended to show the world through this record-breaking exposition that it would have to be dealt with. The theme of the Expo was "Better city, better life," with five subthemes that revealed Chinese ambitions in the modern era: the fusion of cultures in the city, the prosperity of the urban economy, technical and scientific innovation in cities, the remodeling of urban communities, and the interaction between cities and countryside.

There was no doubt that the Shanghai Expo, with its universal mission and its unique geographic location at the heart of the foremost city in China, aimed to show the world what the nation was capable of in the domains that count: architecture, infrastructure, urban planning, the environment, urban transport, technology, culture, and, of course, sustainable development. However, it attained its goal only partially with regard to foreign visitors (who were scarce, accounting for fewer than 5 percent of the total visitors).

Indeed, the choice of Shanghai, a city with aspirations more economic, social, and cultural than political or military, made it the Chinese capital of soft power. Shanghai boasts exceptional cultural and artistic offerings, from the splendid Shanghai Art Museum on People's Square, which houses collections of ancient Chinese art and artifacts (thanks to infusions of capital from the Chinese diaspora), to the Museum of Contemporary Art (MOCA Shanghai), which mounts intriguing, cosmopolitan, and quirky exhibits. China's second city also organizes the principal international film festival in the country, which each year welcomes professionals from the world over. The twelfth annual festival (in 2010) awarded its main prize to the Scandinavian film *Original*. With such a comprehensive list of activities, there is little doubt that China's desire is to conquer not just economically but also through culture and the arts.

THE MEDIA

Since the 18th Party Congress, in 2012, means of communication designed for foreign audiences have been substantially reinforced. The Xinhua News Agency, which is the official press agency of the People's Republic of China, launched a new continuous news channel in English with a particularly evocative name, the China Network Corporation (CNC). Among the goals announced by the president of Xinhua, Li Congjun, were "to offer an alternative source of information to a global audience and try to promote peace and development by decoding the world from a global perspective."

If to these advances are added the marked increase of foreign bureaus belonging to the Chinese national television network CCTV (fifty-some, which feed channels in English, French, and Spanish); the strengthening of *China Daily*, which is available on the streets of London and Washington; the English-language edition of the *People's Daily* (*Global Times*); programs in foreign languages on China Radio International; and even the search engines Sina.com and QQ.com, then all the ingredients and tools of a public diplomacy of major scope that is determined at the highest level of the state and the CCP are in place. The Chinese government's investment in international propaganda is estimated to be about $8 billion, but the results of this expensive effort are very difficult to evaluate.

In light of recent studies on China's image and the country's nervousness about the international press, the assessment is not conclusive. Unsurprisingly, Chinese media have a hard time penetrating the European market. *Ouzhou Shibao* (*News from Europe*) is the newspaper of the Chinese expatriate communities in Europe. There is no equivalent in European languages of the English-language *China Daily*, which has been readily available in the United Kingdom and is now distributed in other countries on the European continent. The television channels of CCTV (CCTV 10 in French) reach very small audiences, and the same is true of China Radio International. The acquisition of European media conglomerates is faintly possible, but the road would be long, in light of the cultural differences and the antagonism toward China in the press sector. The readers of European newspapers will not be satisfied with a media outlet Chinese style unless it clearly proclaims its colors, as is the case with *China Daily* or *Global Times*. Chinese press coverage of the demonstrations in Hong Kong in the autumn of 2014 was subjected to immense censorship, which also applied to the social media, and that has not helped China's image. In Chinese universities (Tsinghua, Fudan, others), journalists are trained in the same schools as future press attachés, no doubt because they will be working for the same employer. In Europe, journalists and government spokespersons do not perform the same work.

The means of communication are evidently diverse; what are their chances of success? A major stumbling block to international outreach through these means is that the social media that are best known worldwide—Twitter, Facebook, YouTube—remain banned in China. "The equivalent Chinese social media like Weibo, Baidu, and WeChat certainly do have an important impact but they employ the Chinese language and thus address Chinese speakers—hence have limited impact vis-à-vis the international community," states Bill Bishop, editor of the excellent blog, sinocism.com.[11] Second, "Chinese communicators" are not always the best spokespeople since they are representatives of a certain political class. Often their post was bestowed as a function of rank rather than of competence in communication. Third, Europeans still have a hard time citing any Chinese brand, despite the efforts of Haier, Huawei, ZTE, Air China, ICBC, China Unionpay, and others to bring their products to international attention.

Finally, while these initiatives reflect an enduring desire to redress the image of China abroad, their inspiration remains a mystery: Is it a matter of wanting to conquer, or even of wanting to exact revenge? Is it the desire to sit at the concert of nations by imposing China's policy positions? If that were the case, then the public diplomacy that seems to have become one of the pillars of China's foreign policy ought to be accompanied by a more comprehensive international strategy aimed at intervening actively in conflict resolution[12] and in diplomatic crises, if not in humanitarian ones. Yet nothing seems to indicate more than a timid evolution in this direction, whether on the Korean Peninsula, in Afghanistan, in Africa, or in the Middle East.

A few years will be needed before it is possible to analyze the impact of a new kind policy of communication, one that is backed with considerable financial support but whose ultimate objective remains uncertain, for China stays withdrawn from many strategic subjects. As Joseph Nye of Harvard University notes:

> China makes the mistake of thinking that government is the main instrument of soft power. In today's world, information is not scarce but attention is, and attention depends on credibility. Government propaganda is rarely credible. The best propaganda is not propaganda. For all the efforts to turn Xinhua and CCTV into competitors of CNN and the BBC, there is little international audience for brittle propaganda.[13]

And what can be said about the absence of democratic reforms? There is no doubt that Beijing's difficulties in this matter have a negative impact on the image of China and its businesses. Even if it is clear that the purpose of President Xi Jinping is nothing less than the renaissance of the Chinese nation, the wearying propaganda slogans about a "harmonious world" and the "Chinese Dream" do not seem to be reaching an audience beyond the nation's borders. Without a true desire to communicate with the rest of the world, China faces a long journey.

APPENDIX: WORLD PERCEPTIONS OF CHINA

APPENDIX FIGURE 1. *Percentages of responses to the request "Please tell me if you have a very favorable, somewhat favorable, somewhat unfavorable, or very unfavorable opinion of China"*

	UNFAVORABLE	FAVORABLE
FRANCE	49	50
UNITED KINGDOM	37	45
SPAIN	50	41
POLAND	44	40
ITALY	57	40
GERMANY	60	34

SOURCE: *Pew Research Center, Spring 2015 Global Attitudes survey.*

APPENDIX FIGURE 2. *Percentages of responses to the question "Overall do you think that China's growing economy is a good thing or a bad thing for our country?"*

	BAD THING	GOOD THING
UNITED KINGDOM	28	57
GREECE	30	52
GERMANY	45	51
FRANCE	53	47
SPAIN	46	44
POLAND	53	26
ITALY	75	14

SOURCE: *Pew Research Center, Spring 2014 Global Attitudes survey.*

APPENDIX FIGURE 3. *Percentages of responses to the question "Do you think products made in China are as safe as products made in other countries, or do you think they are less safe than products made in other countries?"*

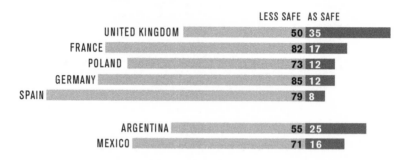

LESS SAFE | AS SAFE

UNITED KINGDOM 50 35
FRANCE 82 17
POLAND 73 12
GERMANY 85 12
SPAIN 79 8

ARGENTINA 55 25
MEXICO 71 16

SOURCE: *Pew Research Center, Spring 2008 Global Attitudes survey.*

APPENDIX FIGURE 4. *Percentages of responses to the question "Do you think the government of China respects the personal freedoms of its people or don't you think so?"*

NO | YES

FRANCE 93 7
GERMANY 92 6
SPAIN 88 7
ITALY 83 8
UNITED KINGDOM 82 9
POLAND 77 11

SOURCE: *Pew Research Center, Spring 2015 Global Attitudes survey.*

APPENDIX FIGURE 5. *Percentages of favorable views of the Chinese and of China.*

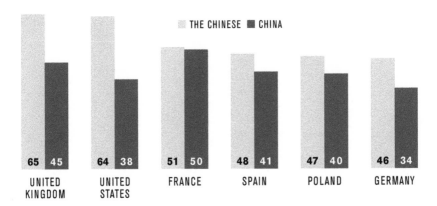

SOURCE: *Pew Research Center, Spring 2015 Global Attitudes survey.*

EIGHT

CHINA AND THE GLOBAL VILLAGE

The internationalization of China, and particularly of its businesses, is one of the most important phenomena of the early twenty-first century. After taking an interest in Africa, Oceania, and Latin America, continents rich in raw materials, China looked at developed countries, and not only for the export of its products or for inbound investment. In the nineteenth and twentieth centuries it was the Europeans who took the road to Beijing in search of cheap labor and a "huge Chinese market," sometimes ungraspable. Today the market is there, and outrageously capitalist, but Chinese enterprises have assumed a broad scope, both at home and abroad. As a result, a reverse feeling of disequilibrium has been developing in the West. Yet the Chinese side sees this as more than a swing of the pendulum. Why should multinational corporations continue to profit from the Chinese market without restriction? Why shouldn't the second largest economy in the world, endowed with unparalleled financial reserves, enjoy rising power in a number of international markets, including Europe?

The economic crisis obliges a deployment of Chinese investments at an international scale that has considerable breadth, in 2014 even outstripping the volume of investments coming into China ($130 billion versus $120 billion, respectively). Despite the stock market crisis of 2015–2016, and the always too-low level of domestic consumption, the fundamentals of the Chinese economy remain good. This book has focused on European countries such as Portugal, Spain, and especially Italy and Greece, which have become favorite targets. The Chinese presence there is becoming visible because it is massive. The three largest European countries—Germany, France, and the United Kingdom—have other attractions, notably small to medium-sized businesses that have not been able to internationalize, but they also have huge corporations that want to remain competitive. Companies like Siemens, Volkswagen, Airbus, LVMH, BAE, and Total are national and international industry leaders that do not intend to be supplanted. For their part, European governments need to encourage employment and the competitiveness of their domestic economy in a context that remains difficult. How, then, to encourage Chinese investments in reasonable proportions?

Partnerships between Chinese and European companies move in the right direction, since they inaugurate a new type of relationship. There is nothing like such joint projects to learn to work together, on the condition, of course, that reciprocity is respected, which necessitates mutual trust. But China, with its single-party political regime, vast geographic extent, and many obstacles linked to the frantic growth of the last thirty years, not least of which is corruption, has not been able to reassure its European interlocutors. There is too much opacity, mystery, and silence in international meetings; too little effort to reform the economy, which remains linked to investment plans inside the country; and still less effort to appear to be a normal citizen of the international community, apart from a policy versed in sensational announcements, such as the "Harmonious society" or the "China Dream," as well as the much more practical initiative "One Belt, One Road." Too often, Western diplomats have observed Chinese delegates who are attentive but very quiet when it comes to making proposals. If it is legitimate, the ambition of the former Middle Kingdom appears to be shaped exclusively by Chinese public opinion, especially when it comes to acquiring European technological jewels. Chinese infrastructure projects directed at Central Asia, the Caucasus, South Asia, and Eastern Europe in particular must be followed by actual deeds. In many countries, too many announcements of cooperation have been made without any concrete results forthcoming. China's word is at stake, and the somersaults of 2015 and 2016 proved that a declining growth rate or a drop in the Shanghai Stock Exchange can freeze the blood of international investors, just as a decline in world markets does. However, shares on the stock exchanges in Shanghai and Shenzhen amount to only 1 percent of the total of Chinese bank reserves. Real estate carries much more weight. It is not the stock market that has enabled a surge in consumption.

Chinese soft power cannot conquer European minds, however, as long as the Chinese regime remains enigmatic in European eyes. The saga of the Confucius Institutes, that unique creation that was supposed to send a message to the rest of the world, has shown that the decisions of the Chinese government are not always understood in the same way abroad. The Chinese civilization is one of the most brilliant in human history, but this is not always the message received by Westerners, who see and hear only propaganda, witness an ambivalent economic model, the socialist market economy, and endure a certain spirit of superiority. However, the state of the environment remains critical in China (despite the Paris agreement on climate of December 2015), innovation is insufficient, and the country is cruelly lacking in new sources of growth. The brain drain and the flight of capital will not help spur domestic activity.

Europeans, for their part, should show themselves to be more flexible if they want to attract Chinese capital. Of course, it is not a matter of modifying social guarantees such as the right to work or the role of the legislature in Western democracies, or even of altering European norms and practices. But Europeans must make an effort to work with one of the most impressive peoples of the past thirty years, who have seen their country pass from great poverty to modernity in an eyeblink. Are European nations ready, though, to concede the jewels of their industry to future competitors in exchange for the takeover of companies in difficulty? Is the West ready to help China acquire the technologies it lacks, as long as the acquisitions translate into more jobs and benefits for European subsidiaries?

The Chinese have undoubtedly used the win-win formula to their advantage, and they have certainly reused it many times. Europe will not escape scot-free from this debate. Europe must accept the emergence of an economic giant from which it has not heard the last word. Between a continent that has long lived on its assets and a China that has no other choice than to internationalize itself, a modus vivendi must be found in sectors where cooperation is possible, and in joint projects (including those conducted on third-party terrain in other parts of the world). In contradistinction to China-U.S. relations, the relationship between the Chinese and European countries is not conditioned by a geostrategic or military rivalry. The EU is nothing like the global superpower that the United States is, which is likely to reassure China. However, Europeans cannot go beyond certain boundaries with regard to social welfare and societal matters. Citizens, unions, and employees would not accept that. Each of the European countries possesses a sophisticated legal apparatus as part of its historical legacy, whether that body of legislation derives from Roman law or from common law. The legislation of the EU adds still another layer of complexity, one that is almost incomprehensible to the new arrivals. However, if they want to be engaged over the long term, potential Chinese investors will have no choice but to understand and accept this system.

Between China and Europe there remain many problems, starting with a mutual incomprehension and a lack of trust between societies. In many cases, Europeans and Chinese have not proved able to work together in a consensual manner. European culture advocates a number of principles, such as the value of individuals and personal responsibility, direct communication, and even the right to be wrong, whereas Chinese culture favors the "middle way," a meeting of contraries that leads to a harmonious synthesis, which does not necessarily look rational to Europeans.

Similarly, European societies are based on the legitimacy of rules and the strength of contracts, whereas Chinese culture valorizes compromise. These oppositions necessitate increasing the opportunities for exchanges and exposure to each other's culture not only on the part of business leaders (as has been occurring for many years) but also at all levels of European and Chinese societies. Ironically, China knows more about North American manners and customs than about those of Europe. This is about to change, with China's rising interest in Europe, expressed, among other ways, in increasing cultural, linguistic, academic, and intellectual exchanges with European nations. Meanwhile, Chinese investments in Europe are proliferating. Countless failures might be avoided if each party made a greater effort to understand the other. And if the Chinese believe they know the United States, the reverse is not necessarily true: therefore, progress in the Sino-European relationship might benefit Sino-American relations, too. After all, the two shores of the Atlantic are closer to each other culturally than either is to the former Middle Kingdom.[1]

In the medium term, there is reason to be optimistic about progress in Sino-European business relationships, since nobody is interested in a dialogue of the deaf. Besides a much-needed bilateral investment treaty, the most promising part of this relationship is the establishment of co-enterprises in Europe, as well as mixed teams that will get to know each other (although first they must share a language and a business culture). Chinese society has changed radically over the last three decades, and there is no doubt that its businesses will sooner or later become permanent members of the global village.

NOTES

PREFACE

1. Ralph Atkins, "Debt Mountains Spark Fears of Another Crisis," *Financial Times*, February 5, 2015.

2. In 2010, the Gini coefficient (a measure of income distribution) stood at 42.1 for China, versus 40.5 for the United States. See "World Development Indicators," World Bank (http://databank.worldbank.org/data/reports).

3. Lingling Wei and Anjani Trivedi, "China's Forex Reserves Fall by Record $93.9 Billion on Yuan Intervention," *Wall Street Journal*, September 7, 2015. The September figure was down from $3.65 trillion in the previous month and down from a peak of $3.99 trillion in June 2014.

4. See the web page www.aei.org/china-global-investment-tracker. At the start of 2016, the same team of experts estimated the total of Chinese FDI in Europe at $147.2 billion.

5. Li Keqiang, "Prime Minister's Report to the National People's Congress," March 5, 2015.

6. David Shambaugh, *China Goes Global: The Partial Power* (Oxford University Press, 2013).

7. McKinsey & Company, *Gauging the Strength of Chinese Innovation*, October 2015 (www.mckinsey.com/insights/innovation/gauging-the -strength_of_chinese_innovation).

8. Richard Gowan, "Red China's New Blue Helmets," *Order from Chaos* (Brookings blog), posted September 30, 2015 (www.brookings.edu/order -from-chaos/posts/2015/09/30-un-peacekeeping-commitments-gowan); Janka Oertel, "How China Is Changing the UN," *The Diplomat,* October 5, 2015 (http://thediplomat.com/2015/10/how-china-is-changing-the-un/).

9. Figures from the 2015 Military Balance (International Institute on Strategic Studies, 2015).

10. Joseph S. Nye Jr., *Is the American Century Over?* (Polity Press, 2015), pp. 60–61.

11. Rhodium Group, "Chinese Foreign Direct Investment in the United States by Congressional District," May 2015.

12. "Taking a Tumble," *The Economist,* August 29, 2015.

INTRODUCTION

1. Perhaps the most telling example was the failed mobile phone joint-venture company between Chinese home appliances manufacturer TCL and the French group Alcatel in 2004.

2. Baker and McKenzie/Rhodium Group, "Chinese Investment into Europe Hits Record High in 2014," February 11, 2015 (http://www .bakermckenzie.com/news/Chinese-investment-into-Europe-hits-record -high-in-2014-02-11-2015/). Chinese investments in Europe include those in greenfields and mergers and acquisitions (M&A) transactions.

3. Baker and McKenzie/Rhodium Group, "Chinese Investment into Europe Hits Record High in 2014."

4. Alicia García-Herrero, "China Outbound Foreign Direct Investment" (Bruegel, June 28, 2015).

5. Eurostat data from June 2014 (http://ec.europa.eu/eurostat/statistics -explained/index.php/Foreign_direct_investment_statistics).

6. French Ministry of Foreign Affairs (http://www.diplomatie.gouv.fr /fr/dossiers-pays/chine/la-france-et-la-chine/).

7. "BlueStar to Buy Rhodia's Silicones Unit," *Techzone360,* November 2, 2006 (www.techzone360.com/news/2006/11/02/2032723.htm).

8. "Chinese Investments in Italy Grow, Reaching 322 Companies," *Il Sole 24 Ore,* June 22, 2015 (www.italy24.Ilsole24ore.com/art/business -and-economy/2015-06-19/chinese-investments-italy-are-growing-with -the-acquisition-of-322-companies—152957.php?uuid=ACDU4XD).

9. Interview with the authors, Paris, September 17, 2014.

10. "From Strength to Strength: EU-China Trade Relations," *Eurobiz,* May 2015.
11. "The EU-China Comprehensive Strategic Partnership" (www.eeas .europa.eu/factsheets/docs/eu-china_factsheet_en.pdf).
12. "Chinese PM Calls for EU Deal on Greece," *EU Observer,* June 29, 2015.
13. Chinese Ministry of Foreign Affairs, October 27, 2015 (http://www .mfa.gov.cn/ce/cesg/eng/jrzg/t1309372.htm).
14. "China Does not Interfere in Other Countries' Politics," *South China Morning Post,* September 28, 2015 (http://www.scmp.com/news /china/diplomacy-defence/article/1862085/china-does-not-interfere-other -countries-politics).
15. See chapter 1.
16. The "16+1" summit is an annual summit between the Chinese prime minister and the leaders of sixteen Eastern and Central European countries (some of which are non-EU members). The most recent one (as of January 2106) took place in the eastern Chinese city of Suzhou on November 24, 2015.

CHAPTER I

1. "Communication of the Commission: A Long Term Policy for China-Europe Relations," 1995 (http://eeas.europa.eu/china/docs/com95_279_en .pdf).
2. "From Strength to Strength, EU-China Trade Relations," *Eurobiz,* May 2015, pp. 12–14.
3. "Deepen the China-EU Comprehensive Strategic Partnership for Mutual Benefit and Win-Win Cooperation," *Xinhua,* April 2014 (http:// news.xinhuanet.com/english/china/2014-04/02/c_133230788.htm).
4. For example, the Europeans, led by the United Kingdom, broke ranks with the United States in March 2015 to join the Beijing-backed Asian Infrastructure Investment bank (AIIB), which was considered a great diplomatic success by China.
5. Statement by Premier Li Keqiang at a press conference following the National People's Congress plenary session, March 14, 2014 (http://www .fmprc.gov.cn/mfa_eng/wjdt_665385/zyjh_665391/t1137475.shtml).
6. "L'UE et la Chine se réconcilient sur les télécoms" [The EU and China reach an agreement on telecoms], Reuters, October 20, 2014.

7. EU and China settle the telecoms case at the Joint Committee, European Commission statement, October 20, 2014.

8. "European Business in China," Position Paper 2015/2016, September 2015 (www.europeanchamber.com.cn).

9. Considered the "flagship project" of the EU-China trade relationship, as it would simplify the twenty-six existing bilateral investment treaties, the Comprehensive Agreement on Investment is currently under negotiation.

10. François Godement and Angela Stanzel, "The European Interest in an Investment Treaty with China," Policy Brief (European Council on Foreign Relations, February 19, 2015).

11. "China 'Speeding-Up' EU Investment Pact Talks to Help Counter Influence of US-Led Trade Initiatives, Say Observers," *South China Morning Post*, December 10, 2015.

12. Interview with the authors, Brussels, February 12, 2008.

13. François Godement and John Fox, *A Power Audit of EU-China Relations* (European Council on Foreign Relations, April 2009).

14. In March 2015, according to the *China Daily* (May 9, 2015), the Chinese government surprisingly announced it would sponsor 10,000 Chinese students to study in France.

15. Institute of International Education, *Open Doors Report 2014* (http://www.iie.org/en/Research-and-Publications/Open-Doors/Data).

16. Only matched, in pomp and circumstance, by President Xi's state visit to the United Kingdom in October 2015. See Philippe Le Corre, "The New Sino-British Relationship," *Foreign Affairs*, October 19, 2015 (https://www.foreignaffairs.com/articles/2015-10-19/new-special -relationship).

17. "Au Havre, le projet Eurasia de Monsieur Wang au point mort" [In Le Havre, Mr. Wang's Eurasia project stalled], *Paris Normandie*, November 23, 2014 (http://www.paris-normandie.fr/detail_article/articles /1939881/le-dragon-eurasia-sans-souffle).

18. Interview with the authors, Le Havre, July 25, 2013.

19. Interview with the authors, Paris, March 8, 2014.

20. Interview with the authors, April 22, 2014.

21. On the strengths of Germany, see the web page http://china.ahk.de /cn/marketinfo-germany/economy-strength/.

22. Although the brand's image is beginning to be slightly affected by Volkswagen's 2015 diesel global scandal.

23. Thilo Hanemann and Mikko Huotari, "Chinese FDI in Europe and Germany: preparing for a new era of Chinese capital" (Mercator Institute for China Studies and Rhodium Group, June 2015).

24. Ibid.

25. Samuel Huntington explored the idea more generally in his study of post–Cold War international relations, *The Clash of Civilizations and the Remaking of World Order* (Simon and Schuster, 2011).

26. Interview with the authors, September 18, 2013.

27. Interview with the authors, October 8, 2013.

28. Interview with the authors, Milan, December 9, 2013.

29. Interview with the authors, Beijing, September 23, 2013.

30. The contract with COSCO, it should be noted, authorized COSCO to offer lower salaries and less protection for employees and unions.

31. "China Seeks Dominance in Athens Harbor," *Spiegel online*, September 4, 2015, p. 1.

32. Yanis Varoufakis made the remarks while he was a guest at the Brookings Institution in Washington on April 16, 2015.

33. Interview with the authors, Milan, December 9, 2013.

34. "China Changes Tack with Huge Bet on European Assets," *Financial Times*, October 7, 2014.

35. Alberto Forchielli (http://www.albertoforchielli.com/2014/09/26).

36. "China Changes Tack," *Financial Times*, October 7, 2014.

37. "The Winners and Losers of Portugal's Golden Visa Scheme," BBC, March 19, 2014.

38. According to *The Economist* (November 22, 2014), between 2012 and 2014 the Portuguese government granted 1,775 "golden visas," corresponding to a total Chinese investment of $1.2 billion. A scandal arose in 2014 involving the misappropriation of money for visas for Chinese "investors."

39. "Chinese Investors Play Key Role in Portugal Success," *Financial Times*, October 6, 2014.

40. For example, in 2012 a large-scale police operation dismantled a criminal gang network.

41. Interview with the authors, April 15, 2014.

42. Interview with the authors, May 20, 2014.

43. Interview with the authors, Beijing, December 8, 2015. The seven MoUs were signed between China and the following countries: Hungary, Bulgaria, Romania, Slovakia, Poland, the Czech Republic, and Serbia.

44. See the web page http://www.ibtimes.co.uk/london-set-become
-first-financial-centre-west-offer-chinese-sovereign-debt-1523873.

45. "The UK-China Experiment," *The Diplomat,* December 3, 2013.

46. "David Cameron Calls for China Investment," *Financial Times,*
December 2, 2014.

47. *Financial Times,* March 12, 2015 (http://www.ft.com/intl/cms/s/0
/31c4880a-c8d2-11e4-bc64-00144feab7de.html#axzz3ucbqMux2).

48. Interview with the authors, July 17, 2013.

49. UK House of Commons, Intelligence and Security Committee report, October 31, 2013. Hansard, Column 335 WH.

CHAPTER 2

1. Evan Osnos, "The Grand Tour: Europe on 1500 Yuan a Day," *The
New Yorker,* April 18, 2011.

2. Savills report cited in Laura Battle, "Where (and Why) the Super-Rich
Are Investing in Real Estate," *Financial Times,* January 17, 2014 (http://
www.ft.com/intl/cms/s/2/595c2656-791a-11e3-91ac-00144feabdc0.html).

3. Report by Knight Frank LLP, a London-based commercial and residential property consultancy, cited in Battle, "Where (and Why)."

4. "Digging for Victory: Construction Equipment," *The Economist,*
December 21, 2013.

5. "SAFE—Un Chinois lorgne le centre commercial Beaugrenelle"
[SAFE—A Chinese eyeing the Beaugrenelle shopping mall], *Le Figaro,* October, 9 2013.

6. "Cooling Measures in Asia Spur Capital Flows to the West," *South
China Morning Post,* May 27, 2014.

7. "A Rail Firm from China Puts a Toe into the US," *New York Times,*
September 4, 2015.

8. "Bienvenue aux envahisseurs chinois" [Welcome to the Chinese in-
vaders], *Le Monde,* February 17, 2015.

9. Manuel Valls, interview on France 2 television (evening news), December 16, 2014.

10. See chapter 7 of this book and the Pew Research Center's Global
Attitudes Survey (Spring 2015).

11. Interview with the authors, January 8, 2014.

12. "Volvo Repairs Flaws in Marriage to Geely," *Financial Times,*
March 11, 2014.

13. "Peugeot's China Tie-up with Dongfeng Targets 1m Cars a Year," *Financial Times,* January 26, 2014.

14. "L'automobile chinoise envahit l'Europe" [The Chinese automobile invades Europe], *La Libre Belgique,* February 20, 2014.

15. Claudia D'Arpizio, *Luxury Goods Worldwide Market Study Spring 2014* (Bain and Co., May 19, 2014).

16. "Chinese Consumers: Doing It Their Way," *The Economist,* January 29, 2014.

17. "Vin: Trois nouveaux châteaux bordelais sous pavillon chinois" [Wine: Three new Bordeaux châteaux under the Chinese flag], *Les Echos,* June 4, 2013.

18. Interview with the authors, July 15, 2014. See also Jeremy Clegg and Hinrich Voss, "Inside the China-EU FDI Bond," *China and World Economy* 19, no. 4 (2011), pp. 92–108.

19. "Démarrage imminent pour la base logistisque sino-européenne Terralorraine" [Imminent construction kick-off for the Sino-European logistical base Terralorraine], *L'Usine Nouvelle,* January 16, 2015.

CHAPTER 3

1. *China Daily,* January 24, 2014, p. 1.

2. "Chinese Billionaire Invests $1.6 Billion in London Land, Yachts," Bloomberg, June 19, 2013.

3. "Wang Jianlin à la conquête du monde" [Wang Jianlin to conquer the world], *Le Monde,* September 14, 2013.

4. With the purchase of the famous Italian tire manufacturer Pirelli, ChemChina seems oriented toward diversification (see "Silk Road Fund Joins ChemChina in Industrial Investment in Pirelli" *China Daily,* June 5, 2015). Also to be noted is the involvement of the new state-owned Silk Road Fund—intrinsically tied to eponymous development—which is investing 25 percent of the capital of CNRC International Holding (H.K.) Ltd. (a company quoted on the Hong Kong Stock Exchange) that, under the control of ChemChina, has taken a majority share in Pirelli.

5. "Chinese Groups Lead Race for Portugal's Novo Banco," *Financial Times,* June 1, 2015.

6. Interview with the authors in Shanghai, July 18, 2013.

7. Stan Shih, *Me Too Is Not My Style* (Commonwealth, 1996).

8. According to the marketing and communications group WPP, in 2013 the ten principal Chinese brands were China Mobile, Industrial and Commercial Bank of China, Tencent, China Construction Bank, Baidu, Bank of Agriculture, Bank of China, Sinopec, Petrochina, and China Life.

9. "Germans Struggle to Name Chinese Brands," *China Daily*, December 17, 2013.

10. "China Economic Plan Calls for Mergers, Public Listings by 2020," *Wall Street Journal*, September 7, 2015.

11. "Cofco Teams Up with Chinese Fund to Create Global Grains Trader," *Financial Times*, May 14, 2015.

CHAPTER 4

1. "Europe: Visible Faces of CIC Investments," *China Daily*, September 30, 2013.

2. "Un nouveau fonds pour les ETI européennes et chinoises" [A new fund for European and Chinese ETI], *CF News*, June 27, 2014.

3. The story is available at http://www.financeasia.com/News/396507 ,carlyle-raises-425m-after-divesting-haier-stake.aspx.

4. See chapter 6.

5. "Industrial and Commercial Bank of China, the Country's Biggest Lender, Will Buy Turkey-Based Bank Tekstil Bankasi," Bloomberg, April 29, 2014.

6. The allusion is to "dim-sum," the steamed, small-portion dishes well known in Chinese restaurants throughout the world.

7. Saikat Chatterjee, "Record Redemptions for Offshore Yuan Debt as China Opens Onshore Door Wider," Reuters, October 11, 2015 (http://www.reuters.com/article/china-debt-offshore-idUSL3N12818T20151011).

8. The situation changed beginning in April 2015: "China Refrained from Granting New Quotas for Residents to Invest in Overseas Markets, As Authorities Were Trying to Stem Weakness in the Yuan," *Bloomberg Business Review*, September 7, 2015.

9. Ian Talley, "China Joins World's Elite Currency Club," *Wall Street Journal*, November 30, 2015.

10. "Frankfurt Picked as European renminbi Hub," *Reuters*, March 29, 2014.

11. "China to Start Direct Foreign-Exchange Trades with U.K.," *Wall Street Journal*, June 18, 2014.

12. In 2011, it was not by chance that the chairman of ICBC, Jiang Jianqing, chose Luxembourg for the official launch of the opening of six new branches in Europe, in the presence of Luxembourg's minister of finance.

13. "Success in Europe 'Takes Time,'" *China Daily*, October 11, 2013.

CHAPTER 5

1. Daniel Vial, former Pierre Cardin adviser, interview with the authors, Paris, February 18, 2010.

2. James Mann, *Beijing Jeep: The Short, Unhappy Romance of American Business in China* (Simon and Schuster, 1989), pp. 76–77.

3. Mohamed Branine, "Cross-cultural Training of Managers: An Evaluation of a Management Programme for Chinese Managers," *Emerald Insight* (online), September 2004 (www.emeraldinsight.com/0262-1711.htm), p. 464.

4. Ibid., p. 471.

5. Interview with the authors, Shanghai, December 18, 2013.

6. John Quelch, currently the Charles Edward Wilson Professor of Business Administration at Harvard Business School, cited in *China Daily*, August 19, 2011.

7. During a visit to Huawei headquarters in Shenzhen (July 30, 2011), the authors heard the company's chairwoman, Sun Yafang, praising the fact the group had "no trade union" (in China), "just an in-house association controlled by the top management."

8. Interview with the authors, March 15, 2014.

9. *La Chine hors les murs* [China outside the walls] (Comité National des Conseillers du Commerce Extérieur de la France, 2014).

10. Plysorol was declared bankrupt by a Lisieux court decision in November 2014: "Liquidation judiciaire Plysorol International" (www.procedurecollective.fr/liquidation-judiciaire/564273/plysorol-international.aspx).

11. "Arsenal and Huawei in Global Partnership," Arsenal.com, January 17, 2014 (www.arsenal.com/the-club/sponsors-partners/huawei/arsenal-and-huawei-in-global-partnership).

12. "Undurchsichtiger Konzern öffnet sich—ein wenig" [Opaque group opens up—a little], *Welt am Sonntag*, October 13, 2013.

13. Interview with the authors, Milan, December 9, 2013. Gianfranco Franci is today (2016) the COO of Lenovo.

14. Interview with the authors, Beijing, July 19, 2013.

15. Gina Qiao and Yolanda Conyers, *The Lenovo Way: Managing a Diverse Global Company for Optimal Performance* (McGraw-Hill Professional, 2014).

16. Interview with the authors, April 15, 2014.

17. Interview with the authors, Hong Kong, September 27, 2014.

18. Ibid.

19. Interview with the authors, Shanghai, July 18, 2013.

CHAPTER 6

1. "The Rise and Fall of China's Sun King," Reuters, May 20, 2013 (http://www.reuters.com/article/us-suntech-shi-specialreport-idUSBRE94 I00220130520#lc7jS3ezA8BMQmkm.97).

2. "Wang Jianlin à la conquête du monde" [Wang Jianlin to conquer the world], *Le Monde*, September 14, 2013.

3. "Chinese Private Firms Tap into Overseas Markets," *Xinhua News Agency,* February 10, 2013.

4. Richard McGregor, *The Party: The Secret World of China's Communist Rulers* (HarperCollins, 2010), pp. 70–80.

5. See the New Hope Group's website (www.newhopegroup.com/EN /Aboutus).

6. See Zheping Huang, "China's Top Bankers Who 'Disappeared,' Were Detained, or Died Unnaturally This Year," *Quartz,* December 12, 2015 (http://qz.com/570524/a-list-of-chinas-top-bankers-who-disappeared-were -detained-or-died-in-the-past-year/).

7. "Billions in Hidden Riches for Family of Chinese Leader," *New York Times*, October 25, 2012.

8. "J.P. Morgan and the Wen Family," *New York Times*, November 13, 2013.

9. Bloomberg, June 25, 2012.

10. The trial of Zhou Yongkang took place in May 2015 behind closed doors.

11. ICIJ, "Leaked Records Reveal Offshore Holdings of China's Elite," January 21, 2014 (www.icij.org/offshore/leaked-records-reveal-offshore -holdings-chinas-elite#).

12. "Chinese General Guo Boxiong Accused of Corruption," BBC, July 30, 2015.

13. About €4.6 million, according to the exchange rate at the time (1 euro=7.6 RMB).

14. "Huawei va investir 1,5 milliard d'euros en France" [Huawei will invest 1.5 billion euros in France], *Le Monde*, September 29, 2014 (http://www.lemonde.fr/economie/article/2014/09/29/huawei-va-inves tir-1-5-milliard-d-euros-en-france-selon-les-echos_4496597_3234 .html).

15. Report by the Special Representative on Cybersecurity, French Senate, July 18, 2012.

16. For example, "Démontage d'équipements Huawei et ZTE outremer" [Dismantling of Huawei and ZTE equipment overseas], *Les Echos*, October 23, 2013. ANSSI, the French National Agency for Security of Information Systems, reports to the General Secretariat of National Defense and Security in the office of the French prime minister.

CHAPTER 7

1. David Shambaugh, *China Goes Global: The Partial Power* (Oxford University Press, 2013), pp. 45–120.

2. See also Philippe Le Corre "Other Perceptions of China," cowritten with Amadou Sy, Harold Trinkunas, and Yun Sun, *Order from Chaos* (Brookings blog), posted May 27, 2015 (http://www.brookings.edu/blogs /order-from-chaos/posts/2015/05/27-international-attitudes-china-sy -trinkunas-lecorre-sun).

3. Joseph S. Nye Jr., "Revisiting the Trilateral vision," keynote speech at the annual Talloires Conference, Weatherhead Center for International Affairs, Harvard University, June 13, 2014.

4. Hugh White, *The China Choice: Why America Should Share Power* (Oxford University Press, 2013).

5. Kerry Brown, "Treating China's Inferiority Complex," *Europe's World*, Spring 2012. See also *The New Emperors: Power and Princelings in China* (I.B. Tauris, 2014).

6. Interview with the authors, April 9, 2014.

7. Joseph S. Nye Jr., *Bound to Lead: The Changing Nature of American Power* (Basic Books, 1991).

8. "Confucius Says," *The Economist*, September 13, 2014.

9. Joshua Kurlantzick, *Charm Offensive: How China's Soft Power Is Transforming the World* (Yale University Press, 2007).

10. Jamil Anderlini, "China's Mountain to Climb—2022 Winter Olympics," *Financial Times*, August 14, 2015.

11. "China's Internet: Gilding the Cyber Cage," *China Economic Quarterly*, December 2013.

12. No doubt President Xi Jinping's important speech at the United Nations General Assembly paved the way in that direction with an extra 8,000 Chinese peacekeepers being announced by China: "China's President Urges UN General Assembly to Put New Development Agenda into Action," September 28, 2015 (http://www.un.org/apps/news/story.asp?NewsID=52014#.VmzFTHsePaY).

13. Joseph S. Nye Jr., *Is the American Century Over?* (Polity Press, 2015), p. 61.

CHAPTER 8

1. See Jonathan D. Pollack and Philippe Le Corre, "Why China Goes to Europe," *Order from Chaos* (Brookings blog), posted July 20, 2015 (http://www.brookings.edu/blogs/order-from-chaos/posts/2015/07/29-europe-engagement-china-pollack-lecorre).

BOOKS

Abrami, Regina M., William C. Kirby, and F. Warren MacFarlan, *Can China Lead? Reaching the Limits of Power and Growth* (Harvard Business School Press, 2014).

Aggarwal, Vinod K., and Sara A. Newland, eds., *Responding to China's Rise: US and EU Strategies* (Springer, 2015).

Araújo, Heriberto, and Juan Pablo Cardenal, *China's Silent Army: The Pioneers, Traders, Fixers and Workers Who Are Remaking the World in Beijing's Image* (Crown, 2013).

Brown, Kerry, *China and the EU in Context* (Macmillan, 2014).

Brown, Kerry, ed., *The EU-China Relationship: European Perspectives: A Manual for Policy Makers* (Imperial College Press, 2015).

Duchâtel, Mathieu, and Joris Zylberman, *Les nouveaux communistes chinois* [The new Chinese Communists] (Armand Colin, 2012).

EU-China Chamber of Commerce, Position Papers, 2015/2016.

Fenby, Jonathan, *Will China Dominate the 21st Century?* (Polity Press, 2014).

Godement, François, *Que veut la Chine?* [What does China want?] (Odile Jacob, 2013).

Godement, François, and John Fox, *A Power Audit of EU-China Relations* (European Council on Foreign Relations, April 2009).

Kissinger, Henry, *On China* (Penguin, 2012).

———, *World Order* (Penguin, 2014).

Kurlantzick, Joshua, *Charm Offensive: How China's Soft Power Is Transforming the World* (Yale University Press, 2007).

Halper, Stephen, *The Beijing Consensus* (Basic Books, 2012).

Jacques, Martin, *When China Rules the World* (Penguin, 2009).

Le Corre, Philippe, and Hervé Sérieyx, *Quand la Chine va au marché: Leçons du capitalisme à la Chinoise* [When China goes shopping: The lessons of capitalism, Chinese style] (Maxima, 1998).

Mann, James, *Beijing Jeep: The Short, Unhappy Romance of American Business in China* (Simon and Schuster, 1989).

———, *The China Fantasy* (Viking, 2007).

McGregor, James, *No Ancient Wisdom, No Followers: The Challenges of Chinese Authoritarian Capitalism* (Prospecta Press, 2012).

McGregor, Richard, *The Party: The Secret World of China's Communist Rulers* (HarperCollins, 2010).

Nye, Joseph S. Jr., *Is the American Century Over?* (Polity Press, 2015).

Nolan, John, *Is China Buying the World?* (Polity Press, 2012).

Osnos, Evan, *Age of Ambition: Chasing Fortune, Truth and Faith in New China* (Farrar, Straus and Giroux, 2014).

Shambaugh, David, *China Goes Global: The Partial Power* (Oxford University Press, 2013).

Steinberg, James A., and Michael E. O'Hanlon, *Strategic Reassurance and Resolve: U.S.-China Relations in the Twenty-First Century* (Princeton University Press, 2014).

Yeung, Arthur, and others, *The Globalization of Chinese Companies* (John Wiley and Sons, 2010).

Zhu Rongji, O*n the Record: The Road to Reform 1998–2003* (Brookings Institution Press, 2015).

ARTICLES AND REPORTS

Baker and McKenzie, "Chinese Investment into Europe Hits Record High in 2014," *Insight,* February 11, 2015.

Burgoon, B., and D. Raess, "Chinese Investment and European Labor: Should and Do Workers Fear Chinese FDI?," *Asia Europe Journal* 12, no. 1–2 (2014), pp. 179–97.

Colchester, Max, and Shayndi Raice, "Europe Finance Lures China Suitors," *Wall Street Journal—Eastern Edition*, February 17, 2015, pp. C1–C3.

Chalamish, Efraim, "Ownership Restrictions Put the Brakes on Foreign Investment," *Global Finance* 29, no. 3 (March 2015), p. 68.

Chen, Calvin, "Made in Italy (by the Chinese): Migration and the Rebirth of Textiles and Apparel," *Journal of Modern Italian Studies* 20, no. 1 (January 1, 2015), pp. 111–26.

"China: Beijing's Investment in Europe Reveals Long-Term Strategy." *Stratfor Analysis* 9 (2013).

Clegg, Jeremy, and Hinrich Voss, "Inside the China-EU FDI Bond," *China and World Economy* 19, no. 4 (2011), pp. 92–108.

Fallon, Theresa, "China's Pivot to Europe," *American Foreign Policy Interests* 36, no. 3 (2014), pp. 175–82.

Godement, François, and Angela Stanzel, "The European Interest in an Investment Treaty with China," Policy Brief (European Council on Foreign Relations, February 19, 2015).

Hanemann, Thilo, "Chinese Direct Investment in the EU and the US: A Comparative View," *Asia Europe Journal* 12, no. 1–2 (2014): 127–42.

Ibbotson, Sophie, and Max Lovell-Hoare, "China's Expansion by Stealth," *Asian Affairs* 46, no. 1 (January 2, 2015), pp. 68–83.

La Chine hors les murs [China outside the walls] (Comité National des Conseillers du Commerce Extérieur de la France, 2014).

Liang, Hao, Bing Ren, and Sunny L. Sun, "An Anatomy of State Control in the Globalization of State-Owned Enterprises," *Journal of International Business Studies* 46, no. 2 (February/March 2015), pp. 223–40.

Lv, Ping, and Francesca Spigarelli, "The Integration of Chinese and European Renewable Energy Markets: The Role of Chinese Foreign Direct Investments," *Energy Policy* 81 (June 2015), p. 14.

Matura, T., "The Pattern of Chinese Investments in Central Europe," *International Journal of Business Insights & Transformation* 5, no. 3 (2012), pp. 104–09.

Meunier, Sophie, "A Faustian Bargain or Just a Good Bargain? Chinese Foreign Direct Investment and Politics in Europe," *Asia Europe Journal* 12, no. 1–2 (2014), pp. 143–58.

Meyer, Klaus, "What Is "Strategic Asset Seeking FDI?," *Multinational Business Review* 23, no. 1 (2015), pp. 57–66.

Pelzman, Joseph, "PRC Outward Investment in the USA and Europe: A Model of R& D Acquisition," *Review of Development Economics* 19, no. 1 (February 2015), pp. 1–14.

Pietrobelli, C., and others, "Chinese FDI Strategy in Italy: The 'Marco Polo' Effect," *International Journal of Technological Learning, Innovation and Development* 4, no. 4 (2011), pp. 277–91.

Rios-Morales, R., and L. Brennan, "The Emergence of Chinese Investment in Europe," *European Journal of Business* 5, no. 2 (2010), pp. 215–31.

Shan, Wenhua, and Lu Wang, "The China–EU BIT and the Emerging 'Global BIT 2.0," *ICSID Review: Foreign Investment Law Journal* 30, no. 1 (February 2015), pp. 260–67.

INDEX